CASTRO'S CUBA

An American Dilemma

CASTRO'S CUBA

An American Dilemma

by NICOLAS RIVERO

LUCE

WASHINGTON, D.C.

F
1788
C 3
R 5

CASTRO'S CUBA

COPYRIGHT © 1962 BY NICOLAS RIVERO

PUBLISHED SIMULTANEOUSLY IN THE DOMINION OF CANADA

LIBRARY OF CONGRESS CATALOG CARD NUMBER: 62:10759

44075   MANUFACTURED IN THE UNITED STATES OF AMERICA

VAN REES PRESS • NEW YORK

To

RAQUEL, my wife,
who, by her wise advice and encouragement through
difficult years, was a solid rock of support.

G REAT events stir great controversies. The Cuban revolution is the deepest upheaval that has occurred in Latin America since its independence from Spain. It has inflamed emotions and created partisanship such as have marked no other event in our hemisphere; it has brought sweeping economic and social changes, and the emergence of a Soviet-style police state in the Caribbean.

My first concern in writing this book was to present objectively the tragic chain of events which have brought about a communist take-over in my country. This book is essentially an interpretation of recent historical facts and of the forces shaping the disturbed world in which we live.

It has been written with heartbreak by one who once viewed these matters in a different light. Fidel Castro and his ideas for revolutionary changes in Cuba were very close to my heart. I saw in them and him the embodiment of all the hopes of my country's unhappy past. In the precommunist stage of the revolution, it seemed to me that Castro was introducing economic and social reforms which had long been advocated but never acted upon. It is true that the revolution was not waged to change the economic and social structure of Cuba, but only to restore constitutional government. Yet Cuba, as all underdeveloped countries, needed change, particularly in its unbalanced economy, which even in times of prosperity could not provide year-round employment for more than 75 per cent of its economically active population—a higher rate of unemployment than that of the United States in its worst period of depression.

As the revolution became more radical it alienated the upper classes in Cuba and created in me personally a psychological conflict between my ideological identification with the aims of the revolution and my family ties. One of the first targets of Castro's attacks was our family newspaper, *Diario de la Marina,* founded in 1823. It was the second oldest daily paper in the Western Hemisphere and traditionally represented the views of Cuba's most conservative element. My grandfather, Nicolás Rivero, a Spaniard, was one of its first publishers, and following his death in 1919, was succeeded by my uncle José I. Rivero, who in 1941 received the Maria Moors Cabot Award for outstanding journalism in the cause of North and South American mutual understanding. He was an outspoken foe of communism even before the Second World War. My father, the late Count del Rivero, was the managing editor until 1937, when he was appointed the first Cuban ambassador to the Vatican.

However, my belief in the revolution was not shaken by the bitter attacks on *Diario de la Marina* and what it stood for. I sincerely believed that the upper classes of Cuba were to a great extent responsible for the Batista dictatorship. Batista's regime became so repellent to me that in 1957 I resigned my post of Cuban representative to the Inter-American Economic and Social Council of the Organization of American States. From then on I dedicated all my time in the United States to helping the revolt against Batista.

As time went on I began to have serious doubts about Castro's aims. I was shocked by his ruthless character assassination of President Urrutia when he spoke out against communism. After the fall of President Urrutia I was convinced that Fidel was a dictator and that he would tolerate neither opposition nor criticism of communist infiltration in the Cuban government.

My position as head of the Department of Information of the Ministry of Foreign Relations, a post to which I had been appointed in the beginning of the Castro regime, permitted me an insight into the real character of the Castro revolution and its ultimate aims to communize Cuba. After the Mikoyan visit to Cuba I was sure that Fidel Castro had perverted the Cuban revolution and that his aims were to carry forward the first Marxist experiment in the Western Hemisphere. Then I began making plans to get out of Cuba. This was difficult because from the beginning of 1960 it was dangerous for a government official to leave the country without permission and a good reason. The wedding of my son, in Washington, provided the excuse.

Since my arrival in the United States, this haven of freedom to all free men of the world, I have been connected with the Cuban Democratic Revolutionary Front and its leaders, among whom I would like to acknowledge the help extended to me by José Miró Cardona, Manuel A. de Varona, and Justo Carrillo, who have made it possible for me to include in this book some unpublished aspects of the Cuban drama. I cannot omit an expression of full appreciation to Mrs. Agnes Slattery, whose devoted cooperation in the book's preparation was an invaluable help.

The Cuban upheaval, which has brought distress to many thousands of Cubans of all classes, has had far-flung repercussions in Latin America. Castro's efforts at land reform and confiscation of foreign holdings strike a responsive chord

among the underprivileged of this hemisphere. To them
Castro is purely a social reformer and Castroism is the solution for all their problems. President Kennedy's Alliance for
Progress is indeed a blessed effort to prevent in Latin America what has happened in Cuba.

Yet there is still too much ignorance and confusion as well
as deliberate insincerity and blind passion in discussions
about Cuba. Immature university students and pseudo intel-
lectuals who lack the necessary background as to what is
happening in my country still regard the Cuban revolution
as the only solution for the evils of Latin America. But they,
especially the young people in whose hands lies the future
of the continent, ought to know that besides the good intentions of the Cuban revolution—human equality, land reform,
education of the masses, economic liberation from imperialism, housing, and improved health services—there are in
Cuba today suppression of freedom, regimentation of spirit,
sordid political terror, and a complete political and economic
dependence on the Soviet bloc.

For more than a year I saw a revolution that had aroused
the hopes and aspirations of the Cuban people for political
freedom and social justice develop into an ingenuous communist masterpiece. Even the Roman Catholic Church was
not aware of the Marxist aims of a movement that had begun
as a revolt to overthrow a corrupt dictatorship and replace it
with a free society which, although radical in its outlook,
would keep Cuba within the family of the free nations of
the world.

The main purpose of this book is to show how a communist minority under the guise of nationalism and social reform takes over a country against the will of its people—and

that this can and has been done in a country almost within sight of the United States.

As a Cuban, and as a passionate admirer of democracy, I wanted to tell the story of the tragic events in Cuba, so that we may better deal with the hard choices that lie ahead of us.

Washington, D.C.
September, 1961

NICOLAS RIVERO

Contents

CASTRO'S CUBA

An American Dilemma

Death in the Swamps

I WILL never leave this country of mine." These were the words of Colonel Vicente León, second in command of the anti-Castro forces, in his last message from the beachhead on Cochinos Bay, when asked if he wanted to be evacuated.

Colonel León relayed this message from a walkie-talkie a few minutes before he was killed by gunfire from the Russian-made tanks that overran the beachhead. Just seventy-two hours after the landing, the invasion attempt had been completely destroyed by Castro; of the original force of 1,325 men, 1,200 were captured or killed. Very few were able to get back to the United States ships standing by, and the few who were able to escape in small boats they found lying in the bay reported the grim end of the operation.

At two o'clock on the morning of April 17, 1961, the United States-sponsored invasion of Cuba had begun as planned. The landing took place in two spots on the coast of Bahía de Cochinos—Playa Larga at the apex of the bay and Playa Girón at its eastern entrance. This bay is located on the swampy southern coast of Cuba. Only two roads and a narrow railroad bed, surrounded by impenetrable mos-

quito-infested swamps, led inland from Playa Larga and
Playa Girón.

Conditions in the bay were excellent for a commando
operation. The crescent moon had set shortly before dawn,
the tides were right, and the first men to swim to shore reported that there was no sign of opposition. The first difficulty appeared as some 1,200 anti-Castro troops were put
ashore. The disembarking of the heavy equipment was slow
and difficult. Six tanks which were supposed to have been
lowered by davits from the deck of one of the five ships
which participated in the operation were delayed because
there were no davits and the tanks had to be pushed over the
side of the boat onto a flattop launch. Two tanks were dam-
aged in the process.

While most of the invaders were already ashore and in
command of both Playa Larga and Playa Girón, C-54 and
C-46 transport planes from Guatemala and Nicaragua began
dropping paratroopers 25 miles inland. Their objective was
to cut communications and roads to prevent a counter-attack
by Castro's forces.

In the early hours of the operation the invasion appeared
to be successful. The paratroopers controlled the access to
the two roads leading from the high ground into the swamps.
The beachhead was enlarged and pushed inland for 30 miles
to the village of San Blas, which was taken by the invaders
without much opposition from the Castro militiamen, most
of whom defected and joined the freedom fighters. Some
units of the anti-Castro brigade succeeded in linking up with
the paratroopers and a drive began toward Jagüey Grande,
the headquarters of the Castro forces for that area. The
objective of this drive was to secure the airstrip there for the

use of the refugee air force, which consisted of fifteen B-26 bombers based in Guatemala 600 miles away.

What the invaders had momentarily gained by the element of surprise was promptly lost by their inability to cut roads, and the appearance of Castro's tiny air force which was supposed to have been destroyed on the ground two days earlier by an air strike mounted from Guatemala. The Castro air force planes—which were not Russian MIGs as was reported—but British Sea Furies and American T-33 jets previously sold to Batista and inherited by Castro, quickly gained control of the air. Of the fifteen B-26 bombers on which the invaders depended for air cover nine were lost— six by Castro's planes and three by antiaircraft guns.

Worst of all, one of Castro's planes sank the SS *Rio Escondido*, a Liberty ship carrying all the communications equipment, the entire Fifth Battalion of the invasion force, and stores of weapons. Another ship was also sunk by Castro's aircraft, and most of the ammunition went down with it. No boats were able to get to shore after the first day, leaving the Army of Liberation on its own—no ammunition, no water, no food, no reinforcements.

By midmorning it became clear that the invasion attempt was doomed. The anti-Castro pilots tried to stop the twenty-five battalions which Fidel ordered into action. These infantry forces, fully armed with automatic rifles of Belgian manufacture and Czech submachine guns, were supported by Soviet-made T-34 tanks and heavy guns carried on flatbed trucks.

The freedom fighters realized that they were trapped, but they refused to surrender. The paratroopers who had landed 25 miles inland were soon engaged by fire from Castro's artillery, but they succeeded in holding up Castro's battalions for twenty-four hours. The main bulk of the invasion force fought its way through the swamp, striking for the road that was Castro's supply line.

With no air support, and with all the antitank shells sunk with the *Escondido* to the bottom of the Bay of Cochinos, the invaders were helpless to stop Castro's thrust. Thirty-five hours after the landing operation was initiated, Captain Roberto San Román, commander of the Cuban Army of Liberation, sent an urgent appeal to Washington for air support. Unless this was forthcoming within a few hours, he said, the entire operation would collapse.

When San Román's message reached Washington, the chief of naval operations, Admiral Arleigh Burke, and some Central Intelligence officers urged that American fighter planes from a nearby aircraft carrier be ordered into battle. President Kennedy, summoned from a white-tie party, stayed up until the small hours of the morning of April 19, arguing the pros and cons of sending a fighter air support to the Cuban patriots trapped in the swamps of the Bay of Pigs. Still undecided, the President called for another meeting with all his key advisers.

For President Kennedy the decision was not an easy one. The day before, April 18, Khrushchev had threatened Soviet intervention in Cuba. In a sharp and insolent message addressed to President Kennedy and delivered to the American Embassy in Moscow, the Soviet Premier said:

The Government of the United States can prevent the flames of war kindled by the interventionists on Cuba from spreading. The military techniques and the world political situation now are such that any so-called "small war" can produce a chain reaction in all parts of the world. . . . As to the Soviet Union there should be no misunderstanding of our position: we shall render the Cuban people and their Government all necessary assistance. . . . We are sincerely interested in a relaxation of international tension, but if others aggravate it, we shall reply in full measure.

On the same day Khrushchev had a reply from the President of the United States. President Kennedy said that the "United States intends no military intervention in Cuba" but flatly warned that if an outside force intervened in Cuba the United States would immediately "honor its obligations . . . to protect the Hemisphere against external aggression." The President added, "Free peoples in all parts of the world do not accept the claim of historical inevitability for the Communist revolution."

Having decided against United States military intervention, it was clear that the invasion forces could not be saved. It was all over. The invasion force was trapped in the swamps.

On the night of April 19 the President received the members of the Cuban Revolutionary Council at the White House. Dr. José Miró Cardona, chairman of the council, asked the President for military intervention in Cuba. The request was refused. Mr. Kennedy, however, promised them that Cuba would not be abandoned and ordered that a last attempt be made to supply arms to the forces remaining on the beachhead. Just before dawn on Thursday, April 20, cargo planes and two B-26's tried to ferry in fresh supplies. But the invasion attempt had already been crushed and Castro had scored the greatest victory of his career.

The misadventure in Cuba was a great defeat for the Cuban fighters. The prestige of the United States, heavily involved in the operation, suffered a major blow. President

Kennedy's handling of the Cuban crisis was criticized even by the pro-American Western European press. West German, Austrian, Italian, and British editorial writers recognized as natural the wish of any United States government to topple a pro-Soviet regime only 90 miles away. But the consensus was that any bid to oust Castro could be justified *only if it succeeded.*

Castro is stronger than ever—his opposition crushed by terror—and Soviet Russia, with an eye toward communizing all of Latin America, appears ready to give Castro's Cuba the aid needed to make the most of this unique opportunity.

Whether Moscow can make a go of the Cuban economy is still a question. But there is little doubt that the Russians will try to make Cuba—the first Marxist-Leninist experiment in the Western Hemisphere—a showcase for all frustrated and ideologically confused Latin Americans.

The Cuban story is a basic one. It is a shocking tale—and one that deserves telling. For it is important for Americans to know and understand the tremendous events that led up to the invasion so that they may better understand the perils that lie ahead. Make no mistake—Castro's Cuba is a threat and a danger to world peace.

CHAPTER I

Triumph and Tragedy

HAD any political prophet forecast the emergence of a communist state in Cuba at the time Fidel Castro succeeded in overthrowing the corrupt and brutal dictatorship of Fulgencio Batista he would have been relegated to the lunatic fringe.

There were some Communists in the bearded rebel army of the Castro brothers, although not many, and the Communists like almost everyone else in Cuba at the time, were too caught up in the revolution whirlwind to change its course then even had they wanted to. The revolt was waged to overthrow a corrupt dictatorship. Fidel Castro, from his hideout in the mountains of the Sierra Maestra in eastern Cuba, had early pledged himself to give the Cuban people freedom and social justice. His first statement the day after Batista fled the country was that one of the first acts of the revolutionary government would be to restore freedom and constitutional guarantees of liberty.

At the time the communization of Cuba was remote, although the Communists, like everyone else, tried to get aboard the Castro bandwagon.

Fidel Castro was the national liberator and as such was widely acclaimed throughout the country. His victory march to Havana from Santiago de Cuba, along a 590-mile route, was in fact reminiscent of the ancient Roman triumph. Fidel headed a huge caravan composed of three or four hundred barbudos (bearded ones), veterans of the Sierra Maestra, and units of the old Batista army which went over to him when Batista fled the country. Army detachments joined the victory parade in every town along its route. More than fifteen thousand former Batista soldiers, with officers and complete military equipment, trucks, tanks, jeeps and army cars, took part in the rebel march of triumph.

Castro made his victorious entrance into Havana on January 8, 1959. Never in the history of Cuba has anyone received such a tumultuous welcome. Crowds gathered along the entire route to the presidential palace, where Castro stopped to greet President Manuel Urrutia and his Cabinet, then proceeded to Camp Columbia, symbol of the military might of Batista. I was in Camp Columbia in the reviewing stand when Castro arrived, and was sitting next to President Prío and Mr. and Mrs. Herbert Matthews of the *New York Times*.

Castro rode into the camp in the early evening hours carrying his famous telescopic rifle over his shoulder. Almost immediately he began to talk to the people of Cuba over a national television and radio hookup. As he spoke, someone in the crowd released two white doves, and one of them perched on Fidel's shoulder where it remained for about an hour much to the delight of the crowd, which interpreted the incident as a good omen. With the four-hour Camp Columbia speech a new era began for the people of Cuba, who were blessedly unaware of what was in store for them.

It was my impression and that of many others who heard and saw him at Camp Columbia that evening that Fidel had that rare gift, which nature seems to bestow impartially on both good and bad men, of being able to sway popular feeling and emotions at will.

After the long dark years of dictatorship, Cuba again became a cheerful country. Havana, where I first met Castro under far different circumstances, was again a gay and relaxed city; the people were joyful and no longer afraid to talk; the press, muzzled for so long, was again free. Castro's bearded, gun-toting partisans swarmed through the streets and the lobbies of the swank hotels, looking like brigands and acting like school children. Most of them were peasants from the back country, and to them Fidel was next to God. They were the humble heroes of a revolution they did not understand, and they were so imbued with the spirit of honesty of the revolution that no one could even buy them a meal or a drink. Such offers of hospitality were refused with the reply, "Thank you very much, but Fidel said No."

It was indeed a unique revolution—a disciplined one, and with great respect for public order. There were no police, but traffic moved smoothly and swiftly; crime was hard to find— perhaps, as they used to say, because all the crooks were in the Batista police force. In those days Fidel was indeed Mr. Cuba. Wherever he went—and he was all over Havana day and night—he was surrounded by hysterical crowds. When I accompanied him one evening through the luxurious lobby of the Havana Hilton Hotel, it took us hours to reach the door. He listened to anyone with a question to ask. He was exhausted and hoarse, but sustained by the inner energy of the genuine political leader.

While the long victory celebration went on and on, the entire population of Cuba welcomed Castro's first statement on honest government, the eradication of illegal gambling, prostitution, and narcotics. The reorganization of government ministries with their long history of graft and sinecure also was cheered by everyone except those affected. His frequently repeated statements about an agrarian reform law were well received, even by the landowners themselves. The cattlemen gave Fidel almost a million dollars to carry out the agrarian reform, which incidentally he returned when the head of the Association of Cattlemen (Asociación de Ganaderos) strongly criticized some of the radical aspects of the agrarian reform.

A 30 to 50 per cent reduction of rents was joyfully received by the tenants, especially in Havana where rents had long been excessively high and few people owned their homes, but it was naturally resented by the property owners, although this rent reduction was balanced by the lowering of interest on mortgages to 4 per cent and the reduction in property taxes. As it turned out, this was only the beginning of Castro's confiscation of private property, which took place in October, 1960, under the so-called Urban Reform Law. According to this law, all tenants were declared to be mortgaged owners and for periods of fifteen to thirty years they had henceforth to pay their rents to the government, plus additional funds to provide for the upkeep of the houses.

But in the early months of the Castro government the majority of the people did not suspect a Communist take-over in Cuba.

The so-called "revolutionary justice," which meant speedy trials and executions of the worst Batista torturers and murderers of young revolutionaries, shocked the world but not the people of Cuba. This was understandable. Seldom in history had there been a more brutal regime than that of Batista and seldom have men more richly deserved execution than

those thugs who carried out orders against the revolutionaries. In the last days of the Batista dictatorship it was not
unusual to find bullet-ridden bodies of young boys who had
been killed in the police stations. In the police torture cham-
bers sadist police were free to indulge in perversions such as
cannot be put into print. Revolting crimes had been committed on the bodies of the victims, and wives were ravished
before the eyes of their husbands.

In the very early days of Castro's take-over, some of the
Batista assassins were even executed without benefit of trial.
Raúl Castro, Fidel's brother and commander of one of the
most important segments of the rebel army, ordered the
execution of more than seventy-five notorious Batista assassins who were rounded up in Santiago de Cuba, the second
largest city in Cuba, immediately after the fall of the dictatorship. They were taken in trucks to Campo de Tiro firing range
near Santiago. It was a mass execution and they fell back
into a trench forty feet long, fifty feet wide, and fifty feet
deep, which had been dug for them by bulldozers.

This brought a storm of protest from abroad. Senator
Wayne Morse, who had been one of the stanchest supporters
of the Cuban revolution, protested, as did many other United
States senators and representatives. The Argentine Congress
went so far as to approve a resolution calling for a halt to
the executions. Old hemisphere friends of the Cuban revolution, like former President José Figueres of Costa Rica,
Governor Muñoz Marín of Puerto Rico, and Uruguay's representative to the United Nations, Professor Enrique Rodríguez Fábrega protested.

Castro was angered and puzzled by the reaction to his
revolutionary justice. He invited more than five hundred
newspapermen to come to Cuba, all expenses paid, to see

revolutionary justice in action. This enormous invitation was called "Operation Truth" and its purpose was to convince world opinion that those who were to be executed were hideous murderers and perpetrators of the most revolting crimes —not merely followers of Batista.

But Operation Truth backfired. The first trial to be held, coinciding with the opening of Operation Truth, was that of Captain Jesús Sosa Blanco, a fifty-one-year-old Batista soldier. He was a brutal killer and was charged with fifty-six murders. The trial took place at Havana's Sports Palace, was open to the public, and was attended by thousands of people. It was held in a style reminiscent of the Coliseum. The people yelled "Kill him, kill him." The president of the court was compelled to admonish the crowd several times and once requested them not to throw pop bottles. The defendant said, "This is the Coliseum of Rome and not a military court." The trial was suspended and from then on all trials were closed to the public and only newspapermen and officials were invited to attend.

Another travesty on justice was the case of the twenty army pilots and twenty bombardiers charged with genocide for bombing and strafing open towns in rebel-held Oriente Province, while Castro was fighting in the mountains. They were acquitted by the rebel court. Under Castro's order the decision was overruled. The chief of the tribunal, Major Félix Peña, was called to Havana and committed suicide. Other members of the court deserted, and a new tribunal was appointed by Castro to again court-martial the defendants. The new verdict gave thirty years of hard labor to the pilots and lesser terms to the nonpilots. Only two were acquitted.

While revolutionary justice was being administered all

over the island, the responsible people of Cuba watched the anti-United States tirades of Castro with growing concern. From the very beginning of his regime Castro bitterly attacked the United States in public. I was in the lobby of the Havana Hilton Hotel with a group of newspapermen, government officials, and barbudos when someone asked Fidel whether he had read in a United States national magazine an implied threat that "intervention is not a thing of the past." "Yes, I did," indignantly replied Castro, "but if there should be one [intervention] two hundred thousand gringos will be killed." The story hit the headlines of all United States newspapers the next day.

I also remember what Castro said in one of his earliest mass meetings in front of the presidential palace, which I attended in the capacity of press officer of the Foreign Ministry—a meeting called to support Castro's stand on the summary court trials and executions. He said, "The criminals that we will shoot will not number more than four hundred. That is, more or less, one criminal for each thousand men, women, and children assassinated in Hiroshima and Nagasaki by the atom bomb."

To a great many Cubans these frequent anti-United States tirades were disturbing, as they feared reprisal measures in the Cuban sugar quota. These fears materialized when in July, 1960, President Eisenhower suspended the Cuban sugar quota. Before that, Cuba had been selling to the United States about 3 million tons of sugar a year at a premium price of 2 cents above the world market. From its 1959 sales of sugar to the United States, Castro's Cuba received approximately $350 million, of which $150 million represented the quota premium price.

President Eisenhower's decision to suspend the Cuban

sugar quota was taken when it became clear that Fidel Castro had passed the point of no return in his journey toward communism. Castro came to power on January 1, 1959, and during that entire year trade between the United States and Cuba was normal. A year later the Cuban government began taking a series of steps that left no doubt that the Castro regime planned a complete change in its foreign trade policy. In February of 1960 the Vice-Prime Minister of the Soviet Union, Anastas I. Mikoyan, went to Cuba to open a Soviet industrial exposition in Havana, and while there concluded a bilateral agreement between his country and Cuba in which sugar was the prime commodity. Since then Cuba has tied her economy to that of the communist bloc of nations through barter agreements. It is important to note that most of these agreements were negotiated long before President Eisenhower curtailed the Cuban sugar quota.

Long anti-United States speeches were not the only disturbing signs in the early days of Castro's government. Fidel's determination not to hold elections, symbolized by his remark "Elecciones, ¿para qué?" (Elections? For what?) created anxiety among the responsible people of Cuba, which included many officials of the revolutionary regime who had fought in the hills with the rebels. In all his statements and manifestos Castro had promised to hold elections within a year, but once he took over he avoided the election issue. He claimed that the Cuban revolution had become so dynamic and had such vast popular consent that he could not interrupt the revolutionary process, whose ultimate goal was to establish a real democracy based on the direct mandate of the people. He also maintained that the people themselves did not want elections because in the past elections had merely meant to them the coming into government of corrupt politicians seeking the spoils of power.

From its very inception Castro's "democracy" was not that of representative democracy with a multiple-party system and related rights of free press, assembly, speech, and religion. Instead, it was a transformation of a semicolonial capitalist economy into a diversified and industrialized one. This new concept of democracy is exactly the same as that followed by the radical leaders of the new nations of Southeast Asia, the Middle East, and Africa. But Castro's concept of democracy was not shared by those noncommunist Cubans who had supported him in the belief that he was fighting for the re-establishment of democratic institutions in Cuba.

I was astonished one day when I heard Raúl Castro, chief of the Revolutionary Armed Forces, say that elections should be suspended for at least ten years in order to give the revolutionary government time to uproot obsolete concepts of freedom and democracy from the minds of the people.

Another suspicious sign of Fidel Castro's ultimate aims was his behavior on a visit to Venezuela. Shortly after he took power he was invited to Venezuela by Rear Admiral Wolfgang Larrazabal, who had been chief of the junta that took over after the overthrow in 1958 of the dictatorship of General Marcos Pérez Jiménez. During that visit Castro made public ostentation of his friendship for both the Communists and former President Larrazabal, who at the time was the defeated presidential candidate, but not toward President-elect Rómulo Betancourt, who had won the presidency in an election despite the opposition of the Venezuelan Communist party.

Some of the people who went to Venezuela with Castro afterward told me that he had some major disagreement with

President Betancourt concerning the exclusion of the Communists in any attempt to overthrow the remaining dictatorships in the Caribbean—the Nicaragua regime of President Luis Somoza and the violent, brutal, and absolute tyranny of Generalissimo Rafael L. Trujillo, machine-gunned and killed by a group of his enemies on May 31, 1961.

On this visit to Venezuela Fidel not only argued with President Betancourt about the role of the Communists in bringing down the dictatorship but also bitterly attacked the United States foreign policy, and even went so far as to suggest that Puerto Rico should be "liberated" from the yoke of Yankee colonialism.

The entire democratic left in Latin America was disturbed by the views expressed by Castro at Caracas and in all probability they contributed to the anticommunist advice given publicly to Fidel by former President José Figueres of Costa Rica during his visit to Cuba in 1959 as a guest of the Cuban government. One of the members of President Figueres' party was the former Costa Rican ambassador to Washington, Gonzalo Facio, a friend and colleague of mine in the Organization of American States, where I served until I resigned in March of 1957 due to deep disagreement with the Batista administration.

Facio told me he would like to talk with me privately about the views of President Figueres on the Cuban situation, and the next morning I met him for breakfast at the Hotel Nacional in Havana, where we frankly discussed conditions in Cuba and in particular the radical course which Fidel Castro was taking against the United States. We discussed communist infiltration in the government and the possibility that Cuba would follow a course similar to that of Guatemala during the Arbenz administration. Facio stated bluntly that Figueres and all true democrats of Latin America were upset by Castro's statement at Caracas, as well as his increasingly evident communist leaning. Facio said that President Figueres, Puerto Rican Governor Luis Muñoz Marín, and President Rómulo Betancourt of Venezuela were friends of the Cuban revolution, which they regarded as a remarkable victory for democracy in Latin America. He also remarked that the impact in the United States was tremendous, that at last the liberal-minded people in the State Department had the upper hand and that all those facts had contributed toward the consolidation of the Castro regime. But, he added, if the Cuban revolution became communist, then the whole situation would change; the United States government would be forced ultimately to intervene, and consequently the people who considered Latin America unprepared for democracy would again gain influence. Facio also told me that he knew from the American ambassador in Costa Rica that the United States probably already had plans for an invasion of Cuba in the event it became necessary.

I was very disturbed by this conversation and made a memorandum of it for the Foreign Minister, Roberto Agramonte, sending a copy to Undersecretary of State Eric Agüero. I never received any comment from either of them, even after President Figueres spoke more or less along the same lines before half a million Cubans and brought about a grave incident with Fidel himself.

Figueres found himself in the middle of a throng when he spoke at the huge demonstration which had been called in his honor by the Cuban Confederation of Workers. Figueres declared that the Communists were an instrument of subversion of the Soviet Union in the cold war and that in case of war between the United States and Russia the Latin-

American countries should be on the side of the United States. When he stated that Castro was leaning dangerously toward the Communists he was angrily interrupted by David Salvador, secretary-general of the Cuban Confederation of Workers.

When Figueres finished his talk, Castro answered him angrily. He said that what had happened in Cuba was a real revolution, very different from that of Costa Rica, and added that Figueres, Betancourt, and other leaders of the democratic left of Latin America were not true revolutionaries, insinuating that they were stooges of American imperialism. Castro then made a statement that shocked the whole Western Hemisphere. He said that Cuba would remain neutral in the event of war between the United States and Russia. Fidel was applauded at the rally, but next morning the responsible people of Cuba, including President Urrutia and some high officials of the government, were disturbed about the remark and feared what the future might bring. They were apprehensive, although some believed that Fidel was playing Nasser's game of East against West.

However, the apprehension was relieved when it was announced that Castro had accepted an invitation of the American Society of Newspaper Editors to come to Washington and address its annual meeting.

About a week before Castro's trip to the United States I received instructions to join Fidel's official party in Washington. My instructions were to help the Cuban ambassador in Washington, Dr. Ernesto Dihigo, in the event of any unforeseen trouble. This appointment was very gratifying to me because it meant that I had the confidence of the Castro inner circle, enabling me to participate in a historical event, for the people in Cuba thought that Fidel's visit to the

United States was a great opportunity to present Cuba's case fully to both the people and the government of the United States, thereby improving relations between the two countries.

The purpose of the trip was, indeed, to improve relations. When Castro arrived in Washington his first words were: "I hope the people of the United States will understand better the people of Cuba, and I hope to understand better the people of the United States." The next day he said, "We did not come here to get money—many men come here to sell their souls. We are not that kind of people; we want only understanding of the deep Cuban revolution."

This latter statement puzzled me, as it did other members of Fidel's official party, most of them from the economic branch of the Cuban government. Dr. Felipe Pazos, president of the National Bank of Cuba, and Dr. Rufo López Fresquet, Minister of Finance, were in the Castro entourage, as was also the Minister of Economy, Dr. Regino Boti, and the former Castro registered agent in Washington, Ernesto Betancourt. All these men believed that the trip was a fine opportunity to reach an understanding with the United States on the two most pressing problems at the time—the Cuban sugar quota and the United States economic cooperation in raising the living standards of the Cuban people through a huge program of industrialization.

Although Castro had publicly denied any wish for a loan or a handout of any kind, Fresquet and Pazos approached high United States government officials, as well as officials of the World Bank and the International Monetary Fund. Pazos recently disclosed that the United States government was eager to help.

Castro was warmly received by the government and the

people of the United States. Acting Secretary of State Christian A. Herter tendered a luncheon in his honor at the Statler Hilton Hotel. Castro also had interviews with former Vice-President Richard M. Nixon and with the members of the Foreign Relations Committee of the United States Senate.

I was one of the few members of the Castro party who accompanied him to the closed-door session with the Foreign Relations Committee. He was quizzed for more than two hours on every aspect of his views on United States-Cuban relations. He flatly denied that he was a Communist and stated that he had no intention of abrogating the agreement under which the United States maintains a naval base at Guantánamo Bay in Cuba. I also recall his statement that the Cuban revolutionary government would maintain membership in the Mutual Defense Treaty, under which the twenty-one republics are pledged to the defense of the Western Hemisphere against attack by extracontinental powers. Castro also declared that he had no intention of confiscating foreign private industry in Cuba, that, on the contrary, Cuba needed more investment by foreign businessmen to provide employment for the people.

Most of the members of the committee were pleased with Castro's answers, the one exception being Senator George Smathers of Florida. He was not satisfied with Castro's replies on communism in his government or on the harboring in Cuba of revolutionaries from other countries. "It is clear," Senator Smathers said, "that he [Castro] hasn't yet learned that you can't play ball with the Communists, for he has them peppered throughout his government."

It was apparent to me that Fidel was more cautious when he spoke publicly on the issue of Cuba's position in the event of war between the United States and Russia than when he was being interviewed by the members of the Foreign Relations Committee. At his first press conference, when he was interviewed as to Cuba's course in such an event, he said that Cuba would "honor its international commitments." But when he spoke before the Foreign Relations Committee he said there was no doubt that Cuba would side with the democratic nations, which of course included the United States.

While in New York, his next scheduled stop, Fidel decided to accept an invitation for the opening in Buenos Aires of the so-called "Committee of Twenty-One," a new inter-American economic unit of the Organization of American States (OAS) created to blueprint the "Operation Pan America" of President Juscelino Kubitschek of Brazil.

In Buenos Aires, where President Frondizi was having a rough time with the Peronistas and Communists, Fidel was received as a hero of the underdog and at the meeting of the Twenty-One demanded from the United States a $50 billion ten-year aid program to finance the economic development of Latin America. There was no action on Castro's proposal, although he did receive warm applause from the astonished delegates.

During this trip the Cuban leader also met President Kubitschek, who was none too pleased with his performance at Buenos Aires, for Castro, rather than Kubitschek's "Operation Pan America," turned out to be the main attraction. In every country he visited in South America Castro received big ovations from the masses and the students, and significantly was always asked the same questions as in the United States—elections, communism, and executions.

Upon his return to Cuba the responsible people of the

island had regained their confidence in him, as there were
signs that at last he would follow a more moderate policy
and put the country on a sound political and economic foot-
ing. The executions were stopped. There were indications
that a rapprochement with Washington was in the making.
The anti-American campaign diminished and the Communists were bluntly warned not to interfere in the labor movement.

In those days Castro's slogan was not "Cuba yes, Yankee
no!" but "Cuban revolution was as Cuban as the palm trees."
Another slogan was "Freedom with justice and bread without terror." When Castro was asked to define the ideological character of his revolution he stated, "Our revolution is
neither capitalist nor communist, but simply Cuban and
humanist."

On May 17, 1959, in his old hideout in the Sierra Maestra,
Fidel Castro promulgated an agrarian reform law which, on
paper, seemed reasonable. Landholdings were limited to
3,300 acres in cattle, rice and sugar; to 990 acres for other
purposes. The owners were to be compensated in 20-year 4½
per cent bonds. Each land worker was to get a minimum of
66½ acres. Cuban officials publicly denied that the agrarian
reform was Marxist. They used to say that the same thing had
been done in Puerto Rico and by the United States occu-
pation forces in Japan, which to some extent was true. Fidel
Castro himself said, "No one has any intention of socializing
Cuba. The Cuban people are not ready for socialism . . . we
are only trying to move from feudalism to enlightened capitalism."

The policy of moderation was of short duration, however.
On June 29, 1959, Cuba's air force chief, Major Pedro Luis

Díaz Lanz, defected and fled to the United States, where he denounced Castro as a Communist. Fidel was angered by Díaz Lanz's defection and called it a United States plot.

A few weeks later President Manuel Urrutia fell victim to Castro's wrath when he spoke out against communist infiltration. The firing of Urrutia as president was one of the first evidences of Castro's leaning toward communism and that he would brook no interference from anyone in his plan to communize Cuba.

The whole Urrutia case was ignominious. President Urrutia committed the unforgivable crime of speaking out against communism without Castro's approval. In a television interview he accused the Communists of criminal conspiracy to take over the revolution.

Fidel remained silent for almost a week. But then *Revolución*, Castro's 26th of July Movement newspaper, came out with a 10-inch high headline: "FIDEL RESIGNS." The story said that Fidel would explain to the people later in the day.

At eight P.M. Fidel made a televised address to the people. He said: "The reason for my resignation is . . . my difficulties with the President, who lacks political tact and a sense of duty."

For more than two hours Castro defamed the man he had picked to be the President of Cuba. Castro attacked Urrutia by innuendo. He said that the President was slow in signing into law most of the revolutionary government's measures. "What's been going on in the palace [Cuba's White House] borders on treason," stated Castro. Referring to Urrutia's stand on communism, Castro said, "Suspiciously he has sided with Díaz Lanz and the anti-Communists."

"Perhaps," Fidel remarked, smiling, "he [Urrutia] can find

ministers in the United States and form another government. It takes only fifteen American agents and the blessing of the monopolies . . ."

Fidel's ruthless character assassination of Urrutia was unnecessary. The President had offered to resign. But Castro ignored it, and decided to humiliate him publicly. While Castro talked, angry crowds gathered in front of the palace shouting for Urrutia's head. The President fled by a side door with his wife and children to avoid the mob.

The outrageous removal of Urrutia shocked those in Cuba and abroad who had taken Fidel's promises of liberty to heart. Many of them began to realize that a new dictatorship was emerging in Cuba and that it would be political suicide to say anything without clearing it first with Fidel. But very few realized that it was, perhaps, the first step taken by the Cuban leader toward the communization of the island.

It is significant that Dr. Urrutia was replaced by Dr. Oswaldo Dorticós, a former member of the Cuban Communist party and that by October, three months later, most of the noncommunist ministers were dropped from the Cabinet. At the same time Major Ernesto ("Che") Guevara, who had just returned from his first visit to the Soviet Union, replaced Dr. Felipe Pazos as head of the Cuban National Bank.

All this coincided with a shift in the labor policy of the Cuban government. At the congress of the Cuban Confederation of Workers (CTC), which met early in November, 1959, both Fidel and Raúl imposed a so-called "unity ticket" of Communists and fellow-traveler members of the 26th of July Movement. This resulted in the ousting of practically all anticommunist labor leaders from the CTC, including Catholic workers and 26th of July anticommunist leaders. Furthermore, a "purge committee" was established for the purpose of removing all labor leaders who had in one way or another opposed the communist take-over of the CTC. Finally, the congress was forced to approve a resolution calling for the withdrawal of the Cuban Confederation of Workers (CTC) from the anticommunist International Confederation of Free Trade Unions (ICFTU) and its Inter-American Regional Organization of Workers (ORIT).

Another ominous event at that time was the arrest, trial, and sentencing of Major Hubert Matos, military commander of the province of Camagüey and hero of the Sierra Maestra. Matos was sentenced to twenty years' imprisonment, although his only crimes were that he had challenged the infiltration of communism in the rebel army, and requested permission to resign his post. According to Theodore Draper, journalist, historian and editor, who has specialized in international affairs and in the communist movement, the Matos trial will go down in Cuban history as the equivalent of the Moscow trials of the 1930's.

Since then the communization of Cuba has followed the classic Marxist pattern. Political opposition has been completely eliminated. All opposition parties have been driven underground or eliminated and many of their leaders have sought asylum in other countries. Only the Popular Socialist party (the official name of the Communist party since 1944) is permitted to act openly. There is no freedom of the press, radio, or television; all communications media have been taken over by the government. All human rights have been suppressed in the communist manner, and a police state has begun to emerge.

During 1960 Castro socialized virtually every aspect of the Cuban economy and tied it up with the communist bloc of nations. By 1961 there was no doubt that he was making Cuba a Soviet-type socialist republic—a fact which he officially proclaimed on May Day, 1961.

CHAPTER II

The Struggle against Batista

TO understand how Fidel Castro, the son of a fairly big landowner, found his destiny in the leadership of a revolutionary movement that took him to power and sovietized a country 90 miles off the coast of the United States, it is necessary to return to the events leading to the fall of Batista.

Cuba, as an independent nation, came into existence at the beginning of the century as a result of the Spanish-American War of 1898, the climax of many years of bloody struggle by Cuban patriots against the colonial government of Spain.

As an independent republic, inaugurated on May 20, 1902, Cuba has had good and bad governments, elected by the people in more or less fair elections, and two dictatorships. One of the dictatorships was headed by General Gerardo Machado, who in 1924 was elected to the presidency in an honest election. He perpetuated himself in office and ruled as a dictator until 1933, when he was forced to flee the country after three years of bloody repression, assassination, and terrorism. The other dictatorship was that of ex-Sergeant Fulgencio Batista, who first seized control of the island on September 4, 1933, when he organized a successful revolt among noncommissioned officers of the Cuban Army. From then on Batista, who made himself chief of staff, was the real power behind the throne in Cuba, during which time he made and unmade presidents.

In 1940, in a reasonably fair election, Batista was elected president. At the end of his term, surprisingly, he allowed free elections, and his bitter enemy, Dr. Ramón Grau San Martín, was put into office. For the next eight years (1944-1952) the Cuban people enjoyed freedom under the administrations of Dr. Grau San Martín and Dr. Carlos Prío Socarrás. Both presidents were members of the middle-of-the-road Cuban Revolutionary party, generally known as Auténticos.

When Batista again seized power in 1952 through a military coup the government of President Prío was preparing to celebrate the fiftieth anniversary of Cuba as a free and independent nation. A presidential election was scheduled for June 1, 1952, and a public opinion poll published on March 1 —ten days before the military coup—showed that of the three presidential candidates Batista was running in last place with no chance whatsoever of being elected.

The Batista coup shocked the Cuban public, and almost immediately there began a campaign of bitter opposition to unseat him. This opposition was led by university students and by followers of ousted President Prío, who was making his headquarters in Florida. Underground organizations such as the Triple A headed by President Prío's former Minister of Education, Aureliano Sánchez Arango, flourished throughout the island.

At that time Fidel Castro was unknown to the Cuban people. He had, however, a police record in which he was described as a terrorist for his activities while a student at Havana University.

Havana University, as were most of the universities and colleges in the other Latin-American countries, was a driving force behind all revolutionary movements. During his student years Castro was known as a hotheaded, impetuous youth whose idealism for political and economic change in Cuba forced him to collaborate with known communist agitators on the campus and with students of secret organizations of a nihilist character, which plunged him into the web of the student terrorist groups.

One of the most controversial episodes of Castro's life was his participation in "Bogotazo"—the riots of April 9, 1948, in Bogotá during the Ninth Inter-American Conference which was meeting to draft the charter of the Organization of American States.

Fidel was sent to Bogotá by a student group of Havana University to attend an anticolonialism, anti-imperialist student congress which was planned to coincide with the Inter-American Conference. According to some of his friends, the expenses of Castro's trip to Bogotá were paid by a student federation of the Perón government. In that period the Perón administration was anti-United States and cooperated closely with communist agitators. It was also known that the international Communists had planned in advance to break up the Inter-American meeting, and during the riots it was reported that there was a plot to assassinate United States Secretary of State George C. Marshall, chairman of his country's delegation to the conference.

There is no doubt about Castro's participation in the Bogotá uprising. It is a fact that he joined the insurrectionists immediately and obtained a rifle from the Colombian Police, most of whom were disloyal to their government.[1]

There have been several stories about the role Castro played in the riots. To some people it was an evidence of Castro's earliest link with international communism, but to others it was just a coincidence. But to all those who wish to present the Cuban revolution as a communist undertaking from its very inception, Castro's part in the Bogotá riots is evidence of the communist conspiracy.

At the end of the Bogotá riots Castro and his companions found a safe haven in the Cuban Legation just in time to avoid being arrested by the Colombian authorities. The head of the Cuban delegation to the Inter-American Conference arranged to have him flown back to Cuba in a plane that had been sent to Bogotá by the Cuban government to evac-uate its delegation should events warrant.

Despite his part in the Bogotá incident, Castro was un-known to the Cuban people until the midsummer of 1953. On July 26, 1953, after a year of recruiting, training and plot-ting, Fidel Castro made a suicidal attack on Fort Moncada in Santiago de Cuba, the nation's second largest city, in Cas-tro's native province of Oriente.

The plan was to attack Moncada at dawn, to take by sur-prise the 1,000 soldiers garrisoned there and, if successful, to seize the radio station and call upon the people to support the revolutionary movement against Batista's dictatorship.

The Moncada assault resulted in a frightful slaughter. Many of the attackers were killed in action, but by far the largest number of them were afterward executed by order of Batista. Fidel and his brother, Raúl, managed to escape and hid in the nearby mountains. Monsignor Enrique Pérez Se-

1 Jules Dubois, *Fidel Castro* (Indianapolis: Bobbs-Merrill, 1959), p. 20.

rantes, archbishop of Santiago de Cuba, intervened to put an end to the execution of prisoners taken at Moncada and was able to secure a promise from the commanding officer at Moncada, Colonel Alberto del Río Chaviano, that the lives of the rebels still at large would be spared if they gave themselves up; that they would be brought to trial—not murdered in cold blood.

Monsignor Pérez Serantes, an old friend of the Castro family, went personally in an army jeep to a place close to Fidel's hideout and delivered him to the army.

The assault on Moncada ended in defeat, but Fidel Castro and his revolutionary movement, which from then on was called the "26th of July Movement," became known to the Cuban people.

At the Moncada trial, which was held in September of the same year in the courthouse of Santiago de Cuba, Fidel Castro became the accuser of his jailers, indicted the Batista dictatorship, and proclaimed the aims of his revolution.

He left no doubt at the trial that his revolutionary movement sought social justice for the unemployed and the farm laborers, land reform, reduction in rents, industrialization, and better distribution of wealth. At the same time he promised categorically that the "first revolutionary law of the nation would be to proclaim the Constitution of 1940 as the supreme law of the land." (The Cuban Constitution of 1940 is one of the most progressive and democratic in contemporary Latin America.)

Fidel Castro was sentenced to fifteen years in prison, but he served hardly a year and a half, as Batista, in an attempt to calm his opponents, granted a general amnesty to all political prisoners.

Fidel understandably did not feel at ease in Cuba after

his release. He wanted to build a legend out of the Moncada attack and become the leader who would liberate Cuba from the Batista dictatorship; but it was not Batista's intention to permit Fidel to build such a legend. On one occasion when Castro was scheduled to speak over the radio the police prevented him from doing so. Shortly after that, he decided to go to Mexico to organize a new revolutionary attempt to overthrow Batista.

Upon his arrival in Mexico in 1955 he began recruiting and training for a seaborne invasion of Cuba. He acquired a ranch near Mexico City covering sixteen miles of mountainous terrain for the training of his small band. The training was under a Colonel Alberto Bayo, a one-eyed Spaniard born in Cuba, who had served for many years in the regular Spanish Army. He had had experience in guerrilla warfare as a captain in the Spanish Foreign Legion fighting the Moors in Morocco. He was also an air force pilot.

During the Spanish Civil War Bayo sided with the Loyalist forces of the Spanish Republic and was in command of the expedition against the Balearic Islands, which resulted in military disaster for the republic. After the Civil War Bayo emigrated to Mexico and became an instructor in the Mexican Military Academy at Guadalajara. According to some Spanish sources, he was one of the few officers of the Spanish Army who became a member of the Communist party of Spain during the Civil War.

Another controversial figure whom Fidel met while in Mexico, and who until this day has had extraordinary influence over him, was Che Guevara, Argentine-born physician. Guevara is now the economic czar of Cuba and one of the most influential men in the Castro government.

There is little doubt that Guevara is a communist agent,

and it is believed that he was planted in Mexico by the Soviet apparatus in order to infiltrate the Castro movement, although there is no proof of this. He was, however, associated in Guatemala with Colonel Jaime Rosenberg, the dreaded chief of the Security Police of the procommunist regime of former Guatemalan President Jacobo Arbenz.

Guevara is now known in Cuba as the Marxist mentor of Fidel Castro, and Number One ideologist of his regime. In an article published on October 8, 1960, by the Cuban magazine *Verde Olivo* (Olive Green), organ of Castro's Cuban armed forces, Guevara stated:

> When asked whether or not we are Marxist, our position is the same as that of a physicist or a biologist when asked if he is a Newtonian or if he is a Pasteurian.
>
> There are truths so evident, so much a part of people's knowledge that it is now useless to discuss them. One ought to be a Marxist with the same naturalness with which one is a Newtonian or if he is a Pasteurian in biology.
>
> Beginning with the revolutionary Marx, a political group with concrete ideas establishes itself. Basing itself on the giants, Marx and Engels, and developing through successive steps with personalities, like Lenin, Stalin, Mao Tse-tung and the new Soviet and Chinese rulers, it establishes a body of doctrines and, let us say, examples to follow.

In an address in December, 1960, in Moscow Guevara said that Cuba stood ready to fulfill her communist-designated goal as a model for armed revolution in Latin America. He also said that Cuba "has taken the road of frontal struggle against North American imperialism" and that the Cuban government had decided to meet terror with terror in annihilating what he described as United States-supported antirevolutionary forces in Cuba.

Guevara, who is now the director of the new Ministry of

44075

Industry, has long been considered Moscow's top man in the Cuban government. He is the author of a book intended to serve as a manual for conducting guerrilla warfare and for carrying out Sierra Maestra-type revolutions in the other republics of Latin America.

Although today Guevara is known to be the communist brain behind Castro and the man who has built the Cuban economic structure along classical Soviet lines, very few people, even in the inner circle of the Castro regime, know that as a Marxist economist Guevara is a very poor one and that in his office in the National Bank of Cuba he received daily lessons in Marxist economy from a young Mexican economist, Juan Noyola.

While Castro was recruiting a revolutionary force in Mexico, other Cubans having no connection whatever with him were plotting in Cuba to unseat Batista. One of these groups, known as Montecristi, was headed by Dr. Justo Carrillo, president of the Cuban Bank for Industrial and Agricultural Development under the administration of President Prío. The Montecristi group worked closely with a group of young army officers who were planning to end Batista's rule through a military coup.

On April 4, 1956, a military plot to overthrow Batista was discovered and its leaders arrested. At the head of the conspiracy was the able Colonel Ramón Barquín, then military attaché of the Cuban Embassy in Washington and Cuba's chief delegate to the Inter-American Defense Board. He had been awarded the Legion of Merit for his contribution to the planning of the military defense of Latin America. Colonel Barquín, with the other officers in the conspiracy, was arrested, tried, convicted, and sentenced to six years in the military prison on the Isle of Pines.

Had Barquín's plans succeeded, the course of Cuban history would have been different, as he was pledged to reestablish constitutional government and call for elections within eighteen months. Dr. Carrillo was chosen by Barquín to be president. All the members slated for Carrillo's Cabinet were distinguished civilians.

Barquín's plans to overthrow Batista started in Washington almost the day following Batista's coup. Most of the planning took place at 6128 Massachusetts Avenue, Wood Acres, Maryland, the residence of Dr. Fernando R. Leyva, a well-known Cuban pediatrician in Washington.

Shortly after Barquín's conspiracy was discovered, another suicidal attempt, Moncada style, was made at Matanzas, capital of the province of Matanzas, 55 miles east of Havana, by the underground organization of ousted President Carlos Prío. Using trucks protected by sandbags, a small group of young revolutionists attacked the Matanzas military post and were shot down by cross fire from the machine guns of the post. After this unsuccessful assault the Cuban military intelligence began an intensive roundup of all suspects in Matanzas, and many of them were executed. Castro had no connection with any of these attempts against Batista but they served to underscore the extent of the revolutionary desire to overthrow the dictatorship.

By the fall of 1956 Fidel Castro was ready to launch his much-publicized seaborne invasion of Cuba from Mexico. On November 25, 1956, with eighty-two men, Castro left Tuxpán, Mexico, on the yacht *Gramma,* bought with money contributed by former President Prío.

According to a prearranged plan, the arrival on the south coast of Oriente Province, near the towering Sierra Maestra mountain range, was to be synchronized with an uprising in

Santiago de Cuba and other places, and November 30 was
the date set for both the landing and the uprising. But everything went wrong. The uprising in Santiago took place as
scheduled, but Fidel was still at sea battling heavy seas and
40-knot gales. At last, on the morning of December 2, the
expedition landed safely at a small fishing village named
Belic on the south coast of Oriente. A few hours after the
landing a Cuban naval ship spotted the *Gramma* and within
an hour Cuban airplanes were over Castro and his group,
strafing them. A thousand soldiers were rushed to the area
to wipe out the rebels. Only twelve of the eighty-two invaders survived.

This small group of survivors, including Fidel, his brother
Raúl, and Che Guevara, were able to reach the Sierra Maestra, where they formed the nucleus of a guerrilla band which
within two years was to become a ragtag army of almost ten
thousand men.

The Batista propaganda machine claimed that Fidel Castro and his followers had been killed. Francis L. McCarthy,
chief of the United Press Bureau in Havana, reported that
Castro had been killed in the landing and credited the news
to a reliable source. The "reliable source" turned out to be
Batista himself.

In less than three months, to the great embarrassment of
the Cuban government, the *New York Times* correspondent,
Herbert Matthews, went into the Sierra Maestra, interviewed
Castro, and took pictures of him and some of his followers.

Matthews' first article was published on the front page of
the *New York Times* without a picture of Castro. There was
immediate reaction from the Cuban government, which
termed the article a fake. The Minister of Defense, Dr. Santiago Verdeja, in a cable to the New York *Herald Tribune*,

called the story a "chapter in a fantastic novel." [2] The next day the *New York Times* published another article by Matthews with a picture of him and Fidel Castro, which prompted the Cuban government to declare that the photograph was a doctored one.

From then on everyone in Cuba knew that Fidel Castro was alive and that an active army of insurrection was afoot against Batista. However, the Castro expedition in the mountains was not taken too seriously by the people in Havana, who believed it would turn out to be another suicidal scheme like the Moncada assault. The only ones who believed that Batista could be overthrown by Castro's guerrillas were the youth of the island, boys and girls from twelve to twenty-five years of age, who joined Castro's underground apparatus. Terrorism flared. Bombs exploded; trains were derailed; towns were blacked out by sabotage of power lines; incendiary fires were started by the young revolutionists. Molotov cocktails were hurled into trucks, government buildings, and warehouses.

On March 13, 1957, a spectacular four-hour attack was made on the presidential palace, with the aim of killing Batista and establishing a revolutionary government. The attackers were Havana University students of the Directorio Revolucionario, an underground organization composed of Havana University alumni and students. Followers of former President Prío also took part in the attack. These revolutionaries had driven up to one of the entrances of the palace in a truck while the guards were at lunch. They rushed the entrance, firing as they went, got inside the building and up to the second floor, but an iron grille stopped them. The

[2] R. Hart Phillips, *Cuba: Island of Paradox* (New York: McDowell, Obolensky, 1959).

battle lasted for about four hours and most of the revolutionaries who entered the building were killed. It is said that the
attack failed because they did not receive the support from
another group that was supposed to have arrived as soon as
the attack started, and which never came. Another reason
for the failure was because the elevator operator switched off
the power on the second floor, thereby preventing the attackers from reaching the third floor, where Batista was at
the time. Neither could they use the stairway, as heavy iron-
grilled gates at the foot of each stairway were locked. Had
they used the bazookas which they had available and had
they come prepared to blow up the big iron doors they probably would have succeeded.

The attack was timed to coincide with the seizure of CMQ
Broadcasting Station in Vedado, a suburb of Havana, where
a group of university students were waiting to broadcast that
President Batista had been killed and his government overthrown. The timing was wrong, and when the group of students headed by the president of the Havana University
Student Federation, José Antonio Echevarría, left the station
many of them were shot down by the police waiting outside.

Fidel Castro was not connected in any way with the palace
attack. Throughout his struggle for power he was opposed
to a military coup, the assassination of Batista, or any act that
would topple the Batista regime, only because he wanted to
do this himself and thereby keep leadership and control.

Shortly after the unsuccessful attack on the presidential
palace, a 26-man expedition landed on the north coast of
Oriente Province. They arrived aboard the yacht *Corinthia*,
which had been purchased in Miami by former President
Prío. The landing was made successfully on a small beach in
Carbónico Bay, about a mile from the United States Nicaro

nickel plant. The landing group was led by Calixto Sánchez White, who had been the leader of the Havana Airport Workers' Union. Sánchez had been forced into exile in Miami when SIM, Batista's military intelligence service, discovered that he had been smuggling weapons into Cuba by air freight, mostly inside of refrigerators.

As was so often the case in Cuba during the long and bitter struggle against Batista, the *Corinthia* expedition was badly planned and executed and the invaders never got a chance to reach the Sierra Cristal Mountains, where they intended to open another guerrilla front like the Sierra Maestra one. They were surrounded by the troops of a nearby army post and most of them were vilely assassinated by order of Colonel Fermín Cowley, one of the most brutal commanders of the Batista army.

Cowley was the military chief at Holguín, the second largest city in Oriente Province. On Christmas Eve of 1957 twenty-six young men were rounded up from their homes by soldiers under the command of Cowley and the next day, Christmas Day, their corpses, bullet-riddled or strangled, were found on the outskirts of the city. A few months after this macabre Christmas present to the Holguineros, Cowley was shot and killed by the boys of the local underground movement as he was leaving a store.

Another attempt that shook the Batista regime was the September, 1957, naval uprising at Cienfuegos on the south coast of Las Villas Province, about 150 miles from Havana. The uprising had been planned as a coordinated effort of naval forces all over the island, together with the help of Castro's 26th of July Movement and the group of President Prío. However, something went wrong: the date had been set but had to be postponed. The Cienfuegos naval garrison never got the word of the postponement. They started the revolt at daybreak as scheduled. The local underground joined them and the city was taken and held for several hours. The Batista troops moved in from Santa Clara, 45 miles away, in army tanks and planes. The city was strafed and many innocent people in the streets were killed. Several fliers refused to bomb the city and dropped the bombs in the bay. Those fliers were court-martialed and sentenced to six years in prison.

General Batista was shaken by the Cienfuegos revolt, for he knew it had been planned as a revolt of the whole navy. He realized that the navy could not be trusted, and soldiers were put on guard at many naval posts. Lieutenant José San Román Toledo, a leader in the Cienfuegos revolt, was horribly tortured by naval intelligence agents and murdered. There was no official record of the exact number of casualties. Jules Dubois, Latin-American correspondent of the Chicago *Tribune* press service, said that a common grave was dug by a bulldozer in Cienfuegos Cemetery and that he saw "fifty-two bodies dumped into it." [3]

It was reported at the time that many of the Cienfuegos rebels reached the Sierra del Escambray, a mountain range to the east of Cienfuegos. There they began to organize themselves for what was to become an active and effective second military front against the Batista army, in which William Alexander Morgan, a twenty-nine-year-old former paratrooper from Toledo, Ohio, was later to play an important role.

By the beginning of 1958 two facts had become clear. One was that the rebellion was too deeply rooted to be ended either by force or by any elections which might be held under Batista. The other fact was that Fidel Castro had be-

[3] Jules Dubois, *Fidel Castro,* p. 177.

come the undisputed leader in the struggle against the dictatorship, although various other groups had participated in both the underground and the guerrilla warfare in the mountains, including a new military front in the Escambray Mountains made up of members of the Prío group and students of the Revolutionary Directorate.

However, the hierarchy of the Roman Catholic Church tried to put an end to the civil war. On February 25 of that year the episcopacy of the Church called for a "national union government" to end bloodshed and restore "normal political life." Batista was annoyed because he realized that the statement implied that he should resign or bring into his government representatives from the opposition. Furthermore, Batista had other plans for carrying out elections without resigning.

Batista appointed Dr. Emilio Núñez Portuondo, his ambassador to the United Nations, as prime minister, believing that Núñez Portuondo as an old politician could appeal to the opposition, quiet down the country, and carry out plans for an election. Batista's plans backfired as Núñez Portuondo resigned when again constitutional guarantees were suspended and a tight censorship was imposed on the press.

Batista took these harsh measures because he wanted to hide from the public the brutal treatment of a fifty-year-old Catholic schoolteacher, Esther Milanes Datin, who was arrested and subjected by Batista's police to one of the most horrible tortures ever inflicted on any woman who survived to tell the story. This outrageous incident became known quite by accident when the Colombian ambassador, Juan ("Juancho") Calvo, found her at the police station where he had gone to obtain the release of one of his countrymen.

By April of that year Fidel announced total war against

Batista and called for a general strike, which failed because of poor organization. The Communists did not support the strike because the Castro underground movement had refused to agree to a communist proposal to form a united front against the dictatorship. The failure of the strike was undoubtedly a blow to Castro's prestige, and Batista tried to make it appear that the rebels were finished. He announced a drive to wipe out the last rebel from the Sierra Maestra and appointed a highly respected and capable army officer, General Eulogio Cantillo, to command the big offensive, which began in the first part of May.

Batista's optimism proved to be unjustified. The drive ended in a rout for Cantillo's forces. One of the main Batista detachments in the Sierra, under the command of Major José Quevedo, an old friend of Castro's from student days, was cut off by rebel guerrillas and after two weeks of bitter fighting surrendered.

This proved to be the turning point in the Cuban civil war. From then on the rebels began to venture out of the mountains from where they operated. By October of 1958 they had cut virtually all transportation between Santiago de Cuba, capital of Oriente Province, and the rest of the island.

In October a column from Castro's army, led by Che Guevara, joined forces with the second-front rebels in Las Villas. Guevara's column arrived in the Escambray Mountains without meeting any opposition from Batista's army.

This lack of resistance was due to the fact that Castro's agents had bribed the corrupt military commander of Camagüey, General Víctor Manuel Dueñas. Castro also bribed Colonel Alberto del Río Chaviano, who was then in charge of the military forces in Las Villas. Chaviano ordered the withdrawal of most of the forces from the places at which the rebel columns were to move toward Escambray and the northern part of the province. Batista was aware of this treachery and summoned Chaviano to Havana, where, during a violent argument, he called him a traitor, slapped him in the face, and ordered his immediate court-martial. It happened, however, that Chaviano was a relative as well as a partner in shady undertakings of General Francisco Tabernilla, chief of staff of the Cuban Army. Tabernilla disobeyed Batista's order, and let Chaviano get out of the country a few days before Batista's downfall.

By Christmas, 1958, the situation for the Batista government was desperate. Guevara's forces had already seized Sancti Spíritus, an important city at the foot of the slopes of the Escambray Mountains and were preparing an offensive against Santa Clara, capital of the province.

These successes by Castro's army and the rumor that General Eulogio Cantillo had been holding secret meetings with Castro shattered the morale of the entire Cuban Army, which from then on lost all will to fight. Santa Clara was captured in the last days of December, 1958, and during the early hours of the morning of January 1, 1959, Fulgencio Batista turned the power of the government over to General Cantillo and with his family fled to the Dominican Republic.

Castro's reaction was that Cantillo had betrayed him. He said, "This is a cowardly betrayal," and disclosed that Cantillo had agreed to arrest and deliver Batista and all his henchmen to the revolutionaries. Fidel also stated that Cantillo was trying to prevent the triumph of the revolution. "If he is so ingenuous as to think that a coup d'état would paralyze the revolution he is completely wrong," Castro declared over the rebel radio.

Castro immediately proceeded to notify his commanding

officers on all fronts to continue the fight and admonished the people of Cuba by radio not to be deceived by the coup d'état in Havana. He declared that the fight would go on until the unconditional surrender of Batista's armed forces and called on labor to start a general strike. While the general strike was taking place throughout the island, Radio Rebelde continually broadcast the new slogan of Castro's 26th of July Movement—"Revolution yes, Military Coup no."

Things were not turning out in Cantillo's favor. Most of the army commanders, including Colonel José Rego Rubido, commander of the Moncada fortress, were surrendering their troops to the rebels. In Havana the justices of the Supreme Court refused to go to the palace to administer the oath of office to Chief Justice Piedra, and late on the night of January 1, 1959, Colonel Ramón Barquín, who had broken out of the Isle of Pines prison, swiftly took command of Camp Columbia, Cuba's largest military post.

Barquín bluntly told Cantillo that he had taken command of the armed forces in Havana, that he supported the revolution, and that he intended to deliver the presidency to Dr. Manuel Urrutia, who was Castro's chosen man for the office. Castro had selected Urrutia for the presidency because of the stand he had taken in the trial of a group of young revolutionaries of the *Gramma* expedition and of the November 30, 1956, anti-Batista uprisings in Santiago de Cuba. At the trial Dr. Urrutia issued a famous decision in stating that all the accused should be freed in accordance with Article 40 of the Cuban Constitution, which protected the right to rebel against tyranny.

With the fall of Batista, Fidel Castro found himself to be not only the commander in chief of the revolutionary forces but also the hero of a genuine uprising against one of the most despised tyrannies ever suffered by a Latin-American country. Nothing would have been easier than for Castro to take over the government of Cuba and establish himself as head of a revolutionary regime. But to do this was not advisable, for during his lonely, ofttimes heartbreaking two-year rebellion, Fidel had accentuated that the struggle he was waging against the dictatorship was for the general good of Cuba and not in the traditional manner of the old-style Latin-American revolution—to gain office and line his pockets with the people's money.

The day after Batista fled Urrutia took the oath of office at Santiago de Cuba. Soon afterward he named his first Cabinet, headed by Dr. José Miró Cardona, a distinguished lawyer who had gone into exile during the Batista dictatorship. Other members of the Cabinet were drawn from the ranks of the 26th of July Movement and included several of Castro's guerrilla leaders.

All members of Urrutia's first Cabinet, including Urrutia himself, have since fled Cuba or sought asylum in the various Latin-American embassies. One of them, Humberto Sori Marín, the man who drew up the revolutionary law for the executions of the Batista henchmen, was himself recently executed by Castro's firing squad for anti-Castro activity.

CHAPTER III

The Communist Take-over

WHEN Castro swept into power the Communists were not popular with the masses. Because they did not openly support the revolution against Batista until the spring of 1958, many people associated them with the deposed dictatorship. Prior to Fidel Castro's landing in Oriente Province in 1956, the Communists maintained a position of benevolent neutrality toward the dictatorship. According to well-informed sources, they expected that Batista would turn toward them, as he had done several years before.

In 1940, when Batista decided to run for the presidency, he recognized the Communist party and permitted the Reds to control the Cuban labor movement. He also appointed two well-known Communists to his Cabinet—Dr. Juan Marinello, president of the Cuban Communist party, and Carlos Rafael Rodríguez, who is now the editor of the communist newspaper *Hoy* and one of the most powerful figures in the Castro regime.

In the beginning of Castro's struggle in the Sierra Maestra the Communists regarded him as "petit bourgeois" and "putschist," without a chance to succeed. At that time the official line of the Communist party was that the overthrow of Batista would come not by force of arms, as advocated by

Castro, but by strikes, demonstrations, and other mass action by the working class.

As late as April of 1958, when Castro and his 26th of July Movement attempted to launch a general strike to topple the Batista regime, the Communists were not, at least not officially, behind the armed insurrection. On the contrary, they helped to sabotage the April strike. Mrs. Ruby Hart Phillips, chief correspondent of the *New York Times* in Havana, stated that the day after the failure of the strike a well-known Communist told her, laughing: "Well, you didn't see any Communists get killed yesterday—we keep our heads." Weeks later the Communist party issued an open letter to the rebels, pointing out that the April strike failed because the 26th of July Movement had refused to form a united front with the Communists. It also declared that only with communist support could any general strike be effective.

Shortly after the attempted general strike, which resulted in complete failure and the butchering of many revolutionists, the Communists began to realize that Batista's days were numbered. It was then that they decided to make overtures to the rebels and sent one of their best men, theoretician Carlos Rafael Rodríguez, to the Sierra to pledge wholehearted communist support to the Castro rebels. Thus the Cuban Communist party's first major working link with the Castro rebels was through Rodríguez, an outstanding Marxist intellectual with a nonproletarian background, who is now the brains of both the Cuban Communist party and of the Castro revolutionary regime. Carlos Rafael, as he is known by his closest friends, many of them with no communist background whatsoever, is not only the editor of *Hoy* but also the ideological guardian of the official propaganda of the Cuban government.

The role played by the Communists in the revolution against Batista is debatable. In all probability Castro had the active support of communist agents from the time he was in Mexico, and there is little doubt that Guevara was a Communist and possibly a member of the Soviet apparatus, planted in Mexico for the purpose of exerting influence on Castro. In the light of subsequent events it is possible that Castro had been counseled by Guevara and other communist agents to have nothing to do with known Cuban Communists, or with the party itself, as he would lose the support of the Cuban people. If the Communists had been fighting alone in the Sierra Maestra against Batista, waving a red flag, there would have been no Cuban revolution. The majority of the people supported Castro because they believed he was striving to restore freedom and constitutional government.

While it is true that many lesser Communists had joined Castro in the Sierra Maestra even before Rodríguez's pilgrimage to Fidel's headquarters, there is no doubt that at the time Batista fled the country the majority of the officers and men of the rebel army were noncommunist. Most of the soldiers were illiterate but religious peasants and wore rosaries around their necks for protection. There were chaplains in Castro's army, and some of the officers were members of the Catholic Youth.

The Communists, however, were probably the best organized party in Cuba when Castro finally succeeded in his revolution on January 1, 1959. Within a few hours after the fall of Batista the Communists in Havana, through their well-organized and disciplined underground, seized the headquarters of all the old political parties that had supported the dictatorship, and hung out signs Partido Socialista Popular (Popular Socialist party), which had been the official name of the Cuban Communist party since 1944. *Hoy*, which had been banned by the administrations of both Prío and Batista, again appeared, strongly supporting the new government.

The Communists immediately began to infiltrate both the rebel army and the labor unions. In the army they had the open support of Guevara, who organized, at La Cabaña Fortress, the first course in communist indoctrination for the armed forces. In the labor unions they encountered more difficulty because the reorganization of the unions had been handed over to the Castro 26th of July Movement, whose leaders were practically all anti-Communists.

Old-line communist labor leaders tried to work their way into union posts through some young Communists who had already infiltrated the labor movement posing as Fidelistas. In other cases the Communists agitated behind the scenes, accusing anticommunist labor leaders of being Batistianos.

However, the first communist efforts to capture labor were unsuccessful. The rank and file rejected them and the new pro-Castro labor leaders were anticommunist. All this was reflected late in the spring of 1959 when elections were called. Union elections held in April and May of 1959 put most of the country's local unions firmly in the hands of the anticommunist members of the 26th of July Movement. During the succeeding three months congresses of various national industrial union federations secured control over most of the group for the anti-Communists.

An example of the strong anticommunist feeling of Cuban labor unions was the election held by the Sugar Workers' Federation, which made up about 40 per cent of the total membership of the Cuban Confederation of Workers. Before the election the daily *Hoy* bitterly attacked the leaders of the federation, accusing them of being counterrevolution-

aries. A mob composed of federation members stormed the
offices of *Hoy*, making it necessary for the editors to request
police protection. Similar rows between Communists and
anti-Communists developed in several other unions.

In May of 1959 anticommunist labor formed the Cuban
Humanist Labor Front (Frente Obrero Humanista Cubano),
composed of twenty-eight industrial federations won by the
anticommunist 26th of July leaders. They declared that the
name for this organization was selected to emphasize the
"humanist and anticommunist character" of the labor leadership of the 26th of July Movement. During that time Fidel
used to say that the Cuban revolution was humanist and in
no way communist.

While the armed forces were being infiltrated and the
labor movement was fighting communist domination, the
Communists were trying to undermine the position of every
member of the Cabinet who was known to be anticommunist.
One of their first targets was the Foreign Minister, Dr. Roberto Agramonte, a known anti-Communist. In one of his
early statements as minister he declared that the new Cuban
Revolutionary Government would not establish diplomatic
relations with the Soviet Union. The newspaper *Hoy* immediately charged Agramonte with being a reactionary who
had no understanding of the goals of the revolution. Agramonte was called Ministro Retranca which in English means
Minister of Brakes because of his attempts to put the brakes
on radical reforms.

It is difficult to state precisely at what moment the Communists became a major influence in the Castro government.
Certainly a turning point was reached on July 17, 1959, when
President Manuel Urrutia resigned under attacks by Castro
for criticizing Communists in the Cuban government, to be

replaced by a former member of the Cuban Communist party, Dr. Oswaldo Dorticós.

There is no doubt that from the very beginning a bitter conflict was being waged within Castro's government. It is a well-known fact that Guevara and Raúl Castro had always favored the Communists. Guevara imported Marxist economists and technicians from the other Latin-American countries to work in the National Bank and other economic organizations. Raúl helped boost into office Communists and fellow travelers. The fact is that as early as October, 1959, Fidel began to place the fate of the country in the hands of the extreme left-wing elements in the government.

However, the old seasoned members of the Cuban Communist party were not placed in any key government positions. Even the labor movement remained in the hands of unknown Communists, among them Jesús Soto, who succeeded David Salvador as secretary-general of the Cuban Confederation of Workers. It was not until the summer of 1960 that the old members of the Cuban Communist party came out into the open as collaborators of Fidel Castro. In August of that year, at the Eighth Congress of the Popular Socialist party (Communist), Secretary-General Blas Roca set forth the prospect of "complete union," of "fusion" of all the revolutionary forces "in a single movement." At the end of October, as the first installment of fusion, the Communist party youth divisions and those of the 26th of July Movement merged to form the Young Rebels (Jóvenes Rebeldes). In December, at the meeting of the Communist parties in Moscow, Guevara mentioned the prospect of a "united party" in Cuba. Finally, on July 26, 1961, the eighth anniversary of the Moncada attack, Fidel officially proclaimed that Cuba was a socialist state with a single-party political system—the new "United Party of the Socialist Revolution."

There is no question that the new party will be a Marxist-Leninist monolithic organization like the Soviet Communist party with restricted membership. In a five-hour televised speech in Havana on December 2, 1961, Castro said that the new party program "will be Marxist-Leninist but adapted to conditions existing in our country." He added that the United Party of the Socialist Revolution will not be open to everybody but will be restricted to proven revolutionaries. The party, he said, "will be a qualitative and not a quantitative organization."

An Integrated Revolutionary Organization, called ORI, was set up in August, 1961, to unify all revolutionary groups in the Castro regime into the new United Party of the Socialist Revolution. The ORI, embracing political, military, economic, labor and social groups, forms the foundation for the coming one-party system.

The advent of the ORI and the nomination of Communist party boss Blas Roca as its secretary general—not Fidel as had been expected—left us no doubt that the communist take-over of the Cuban revolution had been completed.

Roca, who has been secretary general of the Communist party since 1938, is a devoted and faithful friend of the Kremlin. All other ORI leaders were old party officials. Not one was from Castro's 26th of July Movement, and not one fought with his rebel army against the Batista dictatorship.

At the recent Communist Party Congress in Moscow, Cuba got official recognition as communism's third most important nation outside the Iron Curtain. Introducing foreign Red leaders at the opening of the Congress, Nikita Khrushchev gave top billing to the old faithfuls, France's Maurice Thorez and Italy's Palmiro Togliatti. Next came Cuba's Blas Roca.

Roca resolutely supported Khrushchev's blast at Albania, and, significantly, was the only Latin American delegate to be invited with Soviet bigwigs to review the military might paraded on the Forty-fourth Anniversary of the Bolshevik revolution.

One might be led to believe from these events that the Communists have turned Castro into their puppet. Yet it is hard to imagine that Fidel will submit to Roca or any party machine. While it is obviously true that the ORI is under the complete control of old-time Communists, it is just as true that the backbone of the new party owes its allegiance to Fidel and to no one else. In the event of any conflict with the experienced cadres of the old Communist party, Fidel Castro would not hesitate to appeal to the rank and file members themselves.

Blas Roca has a reputation for shrewdness and caution, and he is doubtless aware that he could never control and manipulate Castro as a puppet. Roca has candidly admitted that the Cuban revolution has not followed any pattern prescribed by the textbooks of Marxism-Leninism ideology. If the revolution has moved steadily toward communism, it is not because the Communist party has pushed Fidel in that direction, but because he himself has willed it so. Fidel is still the head of the first Marxist-Leninist party actually in power in the Western Hemisphere.

With the leftward swing of the Castro regime at the beginning of 1960 came the experts from the countries behind the Iron Curtain and Red China. Some estimates put the number at 5,000 from Czechoslovakia and Russia, including jet pilot instructors. The first experts to arrive in Cuba were not military personnel but political and economic counselors, apparently sent to advise the Cuban government on how to become a people's republic.

As early as March of 1960 the head of the Latin-American section of the Narkomindel, the Kremlin Foreign Ministry, Mr. Alexander Alekseyev, arrived in Cuba. He is a lawyer-jurist and specialist in the inter-American system. Mr. Alekseyev came with a large group of Soviet advisers to advise Castro on Cuban foreign policy.

I saw Alekseyev, a stocky dark man in his late forties, many times in the Foreign Office conferring with the Cuban Foreign Minister, Raúl Roa, and with the members of the newly created Department of Latin-American Affairs (DALA), which was in communist hands from its creation in 1959. I was told that Alekseyev and Roa held the same views on soft-pedaling anti-United States tirades. He (Alekseyev) counseled the anti-United States fanatic Raúl Castro not to take any action that would open the way for United States intervention through the Organization of American States.

Alekseyev also counseled Castro to expurgate the Cuban foreign service of people of the old regime, and replace them with unknown but reliable Communists. He stressed the point that it was dangerous to appoint a well-known Communist to any key position in the Cuban government, particularly in the foreign service. He in fact vetoed the appointment of several well-known Cuban Communists to important positions in the foreign service and in government departments, including the Ministries of Agriculture, Commerce, and the Armed Forces where both Che Guevara and Raúl Castro immediately wanted to place Communists.

Alekseyev was one of the seventy-eight top Soviet advisers sent to Cuba in the spring of 1960 to help the Castro regime with everything from top-level diplomacy to exploration for minerals. The military experts, including guerrilla warfare experts from Red China and North Korea, came later as a result of Raúl Castro's midsummer visit to Prague and Moscow. While in Prague he expressed his eagerness to make Cuba a member of the Warsaw Pact—the Soviet military counterpart of NATO—a request which it was reported perplexed Khrushchev. Later, in Moscow, Khrushchev agreed that military personnel and experts in guerrilla warfare from the communist bloc would be sent to Cuba to organize its military establishment.

Alekseyev's mission to Cuba was the result of a commitment reached between Cuba and the Soviet Union during Mikoyan's visit in 1960. Before Mikoyan's visit the Cuban revolutionary process was not yet ripe for an open communist take-over and Cuban foreign policy seemed to be aiming toward the neutralist bloc. Fidel Castro was called the "Nasser of the Caribbean" and in the United Nations General Assembly of 1959, the first attended by a Castro delegate, every step taken by the Cuban delegation seemed to indicate that Cuba was becoming a new member of the neutralist bloc. Dr. Roa announced in the UN that "the new Cuba" would draw "closely to the underdeveloped countries of Africa and Asia." Echoing neutralism, Roa proclaimed that "in the chess game of power politics we shall never act as a docile pawn." "We neither admit nor accept," he added, "that we must inevitably elect between the capitalist and communist solutions." Throughout the session his delegation acted and voted like a member of the Afro-Asian bloc.

Thus Cuba voted for the resolution asking France to cancel its atomic tests in the Sahara and took a pro-Arab stand in the Algerian debate, coming out for independence and voting for parleys between Paris and the rebel FLN. Moreover, Roa backed the resolution on the denial of human rights in Tibet, which was strongly opposed by the Communist bloc.

In his neutralist enthusiasm, Castro even called on Nasser —the living symbol of Afro-Asian neutralism—to cosponsor a Bandung-type conference of the underdeveloped countries. To ensure the success of the conference Foreign Minister Raúl Roa visited North Africa and Europe, making it a point to stop in Yugoslavia. He held talks with Tito and Foreign Minister Koca Rovic and arranged an exchange of visits between Tito and Castro "when possibilities permitted." Another mission, headed by Dr. Levi Marrero, then Cuba's ambassador to the Organization of American States and now an anti-Castro exile in Venezuela, was sent to South America to get the support of the Latin-American nations. Yet nearly all the Latin-American governments declined the invitation to attend the Havana conference, and Castro decided to call off the meeting. From then on, Castro began to look toward Moscow.

As Castro shifted from neutralism toward a policy of close cooperation with the Soviet bloc, following Mikoyan's visit, it became evident that Cuba was fast becoming a military fortress. By the end of 1960 there was little doubt that Castro had the strongest fighting force in Latin America. On January 2, 1961, he paraded his armed forces through Havana, equipped with late-model Soviet and Czech weapons; there were 54 tanks, rocket launchers, artillery, and automatic weapons.

Fidel had planned from the very beginning of his regime to make a military fortress and arsenal out of Cuba. As early as the spring of 1959 I remember instructions sent out by the

Foreign Office to the Cuban embassies in Europe to purchase arms for Cuba. Ironically, about a month earlier and just after his victorious entrance into Havana, he made the remark in a television appearance, in criticism of revolutionary students who refused to disarm—"Weapons? For what?"

Castro's first guns came from the Belgians, whose enterprising arms salesman showed him the strong, light FN (Fabrique Nationale) 7.62-mm rifle used by NATO. So anxious was Castro to get the rifles that he ordered 25,000 at double the usual $75 price, plus 52 million cartridges, 2,000 new 9-mm pistols, hundreds of machine guns, and more than 100,000 artillery and mortar shells. At least twelve ships delivered 75 per cent of the order before "friendly warnings" to Belgium by the United States forced a halt. When the French cargo boat *Le Coubre,* loaded with Belgian weapons from Fabrique Nationale, exploded in the harbor of Havana in the fall of 1960, Fidel Castro intimated, even before an investigation began, that it was sabotaged by United States agents.

Belgium was not, however, Castro's only source of weapons. His agents purchased arms wherever they were able to get them, and it appears that they were very successful despite United States pressure. Ten thousand British Enfield rifles, labeled "hunting rifles," were shipped from Antwerp and some $2.5 million worth of armaments were purchased from Italy.

But what he got from the Western nations of Europe was nothing compared to what he began getting from Czechoslovakia, the Soviet bloc's export arsenal. By the end of August, 1960, Czech-made R-2 30-caliber rifles and other arms began leaving Stettin and Gdynia on Poland's Baltic coast in such quantity that Castro's Red-made arsenal doubled in two months, and is now valued at more than $300 million.

Best estimates of Castro's arms are: 150 tanks, 100 of them Russian and Czech vehicles in the 30- and 35-ton class— Soviet T-34 35-ton tanks, and even the new JS-2 51-ton tanks that have night-fighting infrared sights and mount a 100-mm gun, and can outperform anything except the newest U.S. M-103. He has light and heavy artillery, including 76-, 85- and 122-mm field guns.

There is little doubt that Cuba has today the greatest military land force of any Latin-American country. Despite a weak air force and small navy, Castro has at least 30 used MIG-15 jets, and another 8 or 10 of the newer MIG-17's. Before the Cuban exile invasion, intelligence reports indicated that Cuba was about to receive two destroyers from the Soviet Union.

A small part of these weapons has been exhibited to the public in various military parades, but the actual quantity of arms and ammunition in Cuba are known only to Fidel and his close associates. However, he has bragged about the military buildup of Cuban strength by the Russians. The first time he referred to the communist bloc military aid was at the end of July, 1960, when he announced the arrival in Havana of the first automatic rifles from Czechoslovakia.

During the observance of the Forty-third Anniversary of Russia's socialist revolution, which was celebrated in Havana with more pomp and enthusiasm than in any of the Red satellite countries, Fidel Castro boasted, "We have acquired arms, much arms, much more than the mercenaries and the imperialists have imagined."

Upon returning to Havana after a long pilgrimage to the Soviet world, Che Guevara disclosed that the political interest of the Soviet Union is in supplying Cuba with weapons. He said in a radio-television address to the nation that the economic and military aid to Cuba by the Soviet Union and other members of the communist bloc was motivated by the communist political support of the Cuban government in its fight against United States imperialism. He stated that the purchase of 4 million tons of Cuban sugar by Moscow was made at the written request of Premier Fidel Castro and that "clearly we could not ask the Socialist world to buy this quantity of sugar based on economic motives because really there is no reason in world commerce for this purchase and it was simply a political gesture."

Cuba's military buildup with Soviet weapons was officially announced by the United States on October 28, 1960. On the same date John C. Dreier, the United States representative to the OAS, stated that the Cuban government had been receiving substantial quantities of arms from the Soviet bloc nations and that "with the notorious assistance of extraterritorial powers, specifically those of the Soviet bloc, Cuba is expanding rapidly its capacity to give arms support to the spread of its revolution in other parts of the Americas."

Significantly recent arms shipments to Cuba have originated exclusively in Iron Curtain countries and the Castro government has clearly indicated its intention to continue to depend on the Sino-Soviet bloc of nations, principally the U.S.S.R. and Czechoslovakia, to build up its stocks of war material. With Ambassador Dreier's note was a tabulation of the estimated imports of arms and ammunition by Castro from the time he assumed power on January 1, 1959.

There is no doubt that with Soviet help (weapons, technical experts, and military personnel) Cuba is today a military fortress with more firepower than has ever been seen in Latin America. The uniform is the symbol of the Castro regime—50,000 regular rebel army troops, at least 300,000 civilian men and women in the uniform of the militia, thousands of young children and teen-agers wearing the uniform of the Rebel Youth, the Juvenile Patrol, and the Youth Labor Brigade.

However, not only is the new Cuba a military fortress, bristling with hundreds of thousands of militiamen carrying weapons furnished by the communist bloc, but also as much a communist people's republic as any of the European satellite countries. Any doubt or confusion about the Marxist-Leninist character of the Castro regime was cleared by Fidel himself on July 26, 1961, during the celebration of the eighth anniversary of his suicidal attack on Fort Moncada in Santiago de Cuba. He said, to the delight of his honor guest, Soviet spaceman Yuri Gagarin, that Cuba will establish a one-party system like that of the socialist countries.

Nor is there a question now as to Castro himself being a Communist. The bearded Cuban leader had admitted publicly that he is a Communist, or "Marxist-Leninist," to use his own phrase.

"I am a Marxist-Leninist and I shall be to the last days of my life," said Fidel Castro in a five-hour marathon speech in which he also acknowledged that he had concealed his Communist purposes during the struggle against the Batista dictatorship and for some time afterward. Had he revealed his Communist intentions, Castro said, "we might have alienated the bourgeoisie and other forces which we knew we would eventually have to fight."

Those who have insisted that Castro was pushed into the arms of the Communists by Washington's hostility are now placed in a very peculiar situation. Seventy distinguished American college professors, including forty members of the Harvard University Faculty, in an "Open Letter to President

Kennedy" published in the *New York Times* on May 10, 1961, expressed the judgment that "United States determination to crush Castro ... [reached] more than a year ago ... when certain of today's rebel leaders were still members of the Castro government ... made the Soviet bloc Castro's only source of military and economic support ... [and] our Government acted so as to encourage these tendencies toward dictatorship and anti-Americanism latent in any Latin-American social upheaval."

The inroads of communism today are visible in every aspect of Cuban society. Even before the May Day announcement that Cuba is a socialist republic, no one in Cuba doubted that Castro had so closely linked his revolutionary ideals with Marxism that the two had become synonymous in the public mind. And now external signs also indicate Soviet infiltration and influence. Pictures of Lenin and Khrushchev are prominently displayed in the windows of government-owned stores. Newsstand racks are filled with Soviet newspapers and magazines. Posters proclaiming that Cuba is a socialist republic, and its friendship with the U.S.S.R., Red China, and other communist countries, are displayed everywhere. Cigar stores are selling lighters with communist symbols painted on them and small boys run through the streets waving red flags. The hammer-and-sickle emblem seems to be almost as prevalent as the picture of bearded Fidel Castro.

It will probably be a matter of unending argument whether the march of the revolution pushed Castro into militant communism or whether Castro deliberately guided the revolution into its version of communism.

Castro himself was not clear—possibly deliberately—on this question when he boastfully admitted to being a Communist in his December 2, 1961 speech, and stated that he was taking Cuba down the path to communism. He said that in his student days at Havana University he began the first contacts with communist leaders and that he was "completely identified with the true socialism of the masters Lenin and Marx." He also asserted that with the unsuccessful attack on the Moncada barracks at Santiago de Cuba on July 26, 1953, "the revolutionary thinking was completely formed."

To some observers the meanings of this statement is that Fidel in 1953 was already a dedicated Communist. But others interpreted it as meaning something short of outright communism at that time, because in other parts of his speech, Fidel said that, "We are much more revolutionary now than when we came to power (1959)." He also said: "Once I was prejudiced against Communists, but I did not think they were thieves. My ideas were a product of my education and conditioning. . . ."

Some believe that Fidel Castro became a Communist while in Mexico preparing for his invasion or while fighting in the Sierra Maestra and that everything that has happened in Cuba since then had been deliberately planned. Another view is that what happened in Cuba was the result of the land reform issues which brought Castro to the conclusion that the United States was out to destroy his social revolution. From then on, in defense against a United States economic squeeze, he leaned more and more toward the local Communists, the Soviet Union, and Red China, in due time transforming Cuba into a communist state completely oriented with the Sino-Soviet bloc.

There is also the view that Fidel Castro has been a Communist since 1948, when he participated in the Bogotá uprising of that year—Bogotazo, as it is known throughout Latin

America—and that from the beginning the Cuban revolution was a Soviet operation. The fact is that in every detail Castro has so faithfully followed the communist pattern that arguments as to whether he himself or those who were members of his entourage are Communists are strictly irrelevant. Fidel Castro's economic program for Cuba has been just as characteristic of communism as his political program of complete, ruthless suppression of every voice raised in protest. It has emphasized the wholesale confiscation or nationalization of Cuban and foreign private property, giving the land not to the small peasants as owners but to collective farms or communes in accordance with the Soviet-Chinese model.

The turn from "democratic revolution" to communism was evident in the short space of nine months. Those in Cuba and abroad to whom Castro had appeared as a genuinely revolutionary and democratic liberator watched horrified as the revolution became a communist dictatorship.

Fidel has made out of Cuba the first socialist republic in this Western Hemisphere, with all that it implies to every American republic, including the United States.

CHAPTER IV

Was a Social Revolution Necessary in Cuba?

TO explain and justify Fidel Castro's journey toward communism it has often been said that Cuba was an underdeveloped country and that in all underdeveloped countries the economic and social structure must be changed to meet the people's needs for food, housing, clothing, education, and other things that are taken for granted in the United States, Western Europe, and even in Soviet Russia.

Prerevolutionary Cuba is painted as a backward, semicolonial country, in which impoverished and miserable Cuban peasants were exploited by reactionary large landowners and big United States corporations which opposed industrialization and agricultural diversification.

It is indeed true that Cuba needed social and economic reform, a fact admitted officially by the United States government in a 36-page white paper on Cuba, issued on April 3, 1961, by the Department of State, but written in the White House by Arthur M. Schlesinger, Jr., former Harvard historian and one of President Kennedy's closest assistants. Yet the picture of Cuba painted by Castro's propagandists was false. Cuba was a long way from being a typically underdeveloped country. Prior to Castro's take-over, Cuba was a country undergoing development. Its wealth was increasing from year to year; new industries were being established; the livestock industry had attained maturity and constituted an impressive source of wealth; mining was developing at a rapid pace. And at the time of Batista's coup of March 10, 1952, the greatest desire of the Cubans was to have an "honest" government. Public pressure for integrity had prompted the government of President Carlos Prío Socarrás to entrust to honest men the cleanup of two major departments—Education and Treasury. And in the abortive elections of 1952 the presidential candidate of the Cuban Revolutionary party (Auténticos), the government party, was an honest man, Carlos Hevia, an Annapolis graduate of the class of 1919; the principal opposition party candidate, Professor Agramonte, also was an honest man.

Dr. Manuel A. de Varona, former prime minister of Cuba, and coordinator-general of the anti-Castro Cuban Democratic Revolutionary Front, recently stated that it is totally untrue that Cuba needs a socialist regime to solve the poverty among underprivileged classes.

In a letter refuting a statement by Mrs. Eleanor Roosevelt in her column "My Day," that Cuba needed a socialist regime, Dr. Varona said:

Only fifty years after the birth of Cuba as an independent republic, free enterprise placed Cuba among the countries with the highest standard of living in the Americas.

In 1952, Cuba occupied third place in per capita income in Latin America; was second in meat consumption per capita (only surpassed by Argentina); second in miles of paved roads per 1,000 square miles of territory; second in ratio of doctors to population, and third in standard of wages paid to 500,000 sugar workers, surpassed only by Canada and the United States.

In exports, Cuba surpassed all combined Central American Republics and the peso was one of the strongest world currencies on par with the American dollar.

Our labor laws were among the most advanced in the world, granting workers certain rights and benefits which cannot be found even in the United States.

The Cuban people neither want nor need a Socialist regime. What they desire is a political stability and honesty in public administration within a democratic free enterprise framework. The proof of this is that the revolutionary program against Batista, to which Fidel Castro later pledged himself, was based on these popular aspirations together with restoration of our democratic process interrupted by Batista in 1952.

It was also admitted by the International Bank for Reconstruction and Development that Cuba was not a land of oppressive poverty in which the common man had practically nothing. In its "Report on Cuba," 1951, the technical mission of the IBRD stated:

The general impression of members of the Mission, from observations and travels all over Cuba, is that living levels of the farmers, agricultural laborers, industrial workers, storekeepers, and others are higher all along the line than for corresponding groups in other tropical countries. This does not mean that there is no dire poverty in Cuba, but simply that in comparative terms Cubans are better off, on the average, than people of these other areas.

And the Department of Commerce in a 1956 report on Cuba, stated: "Cuban national income has reached levels which give the Cuban people one of the highest standards of living in Latin America." [1]

Cuba's organized labor movement was one of the most advanced in Latin America, even during Batista's regime.

[1] U.S. Department of Commerce, *Investment in Cuba* (Washington, D.C.: Government Printing Office, 1956), p. 184.

Salaries were high, and even unskilled labor was paid as much as $6 or $7 a day. Concerning labor conditions in Cuba, Ernst Schwarz, the executive secretary of the Committee on Latin-American Affairs of the CIO, said:

The Cuban Confederation of Labor has successfully weathered the latest political storm caused by the Batista coup in March, 1952. It has been able so to preserve its unity and strength as a powerful Cuban institution that even the new dictatorial regime has not dared to touch or eliminate it. The CTC [2] has enabled the Cuban workers to set an example to others of what can be achieved by labor unity and strength. Wages are far above those paid in many other parts of the Caribbean or, for that matter, Latin America. In addition, the eight-hour working day forms the basis for every one of the collective contracts concluded by the CTC's affiliated organizations. Modern types of social protection and insurance are provided in laws, public statutes, or union contracts; while funds maintained and administered in common by labor, employers, and the authorities provide adequate means to put them into practice. The sugar workers' union alone, to cite one example, disposes of such a fund in the amount of half a billion dollars, and its insurance covers medical attention, sickness, and accidents during and out of work. The CTC, moreover, has taken up a place of full responsibility within the Cuban community as a whole, and at present develops its own economic program to compensate for the seasonal nature of employment and production in the sugar industry. Today, the Confederation counts more than a million members—with its 500,000 sugar workers constituting the most powerful of the thirty-five national federations affiliated with it and representing every branch of industry and agriculture on the island. The Confederation has drawn every fifth Cuban into its ranks, and has thus obtained a much higher numerical degree of organization in proportion to population than, for example, the much larger movement in the United States.

[2] *Confederación de Trabajadores de Cuba* (Cuban Confederation of Workers).

The labor movement in Cuba is now under the complete control of the Communists and all the unions have become instruments of the Ministry of Labor. Months ago free elements of Cuba's organized labor movement broke relations with Castro, and many leaders are now in prison. Others have taken refuge in embassies of countries which have not as yet broken diplomatic relations with Castro, and a great number have fled into exile in the United States. David Salvador, one of Castro's closest collaborators in the 26th of July Movement against Batista, is at present in prison, and it has been rumored that he will be executed.

Many of the labor leaders in exile are now united in the Cuban Revolutionary Democratic Labor Front (Frente Obrero Revolucionario Democrático Cubano), known by its initials, FORD. This FORD group belongs to the Cuban Revolutionary Democratic Front, headed by Dr. Manuel A. de Varona. What makes FORD especially significant is that it includes some of the most highly qualified trade unionists with first-class revolutionary credentials. Most of them had risked their lives in the revolt against Batista, and they are now taking steps which might lead to action against Castro. Among these exiled leaders are many who only last December led demonstrations of the powerful electrical workers in front of the presidential palace, shouting "Cuba yes, Russia no."

Free trade unionism in Cuba is dead. In its place the Castro regime has introduced factory committees, workers' councils—Cuba-style soviets—which establish the work norms, the schedules, the incentives, and the wage scales. Hard-won labor standards achieved by trade unions through collective bargaining have been cut 50 per cent. Now discipline is the key word. Workers are exploited and local leadership is scared to death. To impel the workers to higher productivity, Cuba's economic czar, Guevara, introduced a plan known in Russia as the Stakhanovite system—a modern Marxist term for the outmoded capitalist practice known as the speedup.

The communist-dominated movement is officially headed by Jesús Soto, a 26th of July Movement member, who has been a tool of the Communists from the very beginning of Castro's take-over in 1959. The real power, however, is Lázaro Peña, an old communist boss who was the secretary-general of the CTC and one of its founders. Peña, who was the most important boss of the CTC during the first Batista regime, has been for a long time the vice-president of the communist CTAL (Confederación de Trabajadores de América Latina) which is controlled by the well-known procommunist leader, Vicente Lombardo Toledano.

During the 1940's Lombardo Toledano became the kingpin in the communist trade-union activities in Latin America, but he refused to join the official Communist party of Mexico, with whom he had fought many bitter battles in the past years. Instead, he organized his own People's party (Partido Popular) in 1947, which did not apparently lessen his position vis-à-vis the top leaders of the international communist movement. Lombardo Toledano and former President of Mexico Lázaro Cárdenas, are the two main supporters of Castro and communism in Cuba.

Under Batista the forgotten man of Cuba was not the laborer but the peasant. The most backward people of Cuba were the peasants of the Sierra Maestra region. In the rest of the island, however, the peasants were much better off as laws protected them from eviction by the big landowners and the thousands who worked in the sugar industry belonged to one of the most powerful labor unions of Cuba, the Federation of Sugar Workers. They were protected by advanced social legislation and they were not communist dominated. Even now the boss of the Cuban sugar workers, Conrado Becquer, is not a Communist, although he is one of the few labor leaders who has backed down before communist infiltration and has become a tool of the Reds.

In order to understand the strength of the Sugar Workers' Federation it should be kept in mind that those who work for wages make up the bulk of the rural population of Cuba. In other words, Cuba is one of the few countries where there is in the countryside a highly developed working class composed of the workers in the 161 sugar mills located in the middle of the cane-growing areas all over the island.

Cuba before Castro was by no means a paradise. There were ugly things too, in addition to the terror of Batista. Almost a fourth of the Cuban population over the age of 10 was illiterate in 1953 and only 11 per cent of the population had had more than 6 years of schooling.[3] The lack of education of the masses, particularly in the rural regions, meant that millions of Cubans could easily fall prey to unscrupulous demagogues such as Castro and his associates.

Although Cuba is considered one of the healthiest countries in Latin America, with no yellow fever or typhus and with malaria practically eliminated, malnutrition and parasitic infection continue to be major health problems in rural areas.

The major drawback of Cuba, however, was not education or health but an unhealthy economy which failed to give employment to about 25 per cent of the Cuban labor force. Cuba's greatest single problem was unemployment, and above

[3] Cuban census data reported in *Investment in Cuba,* pp. 178, 182.

all, seasonal unemployment caused by the annual layoff of thousands of men after the close of the sugar-grinding season —a situation which Fidel Castro intended to correct through agricultural diversification and industrialization.

According to a 1953 census, only about 75 per cent of the Cuban labor force was employed on an annual basis. This meant that on an average day one out of four Cubans who were able to work and wanted to work could not find a job. It is safe to say that this one-out-of-four unemployment figure was normal in prerevolutionary Cuba. As a comparison, it will be recalled that in the worst year of the worst depression in United States history there were about 25 per cent unemployed, which is the normal unemployment percentage for Cuba.

The main reason for this large Cuban unemployment was the country's economy, dependent on the fluctuation of a single crop, sugar, which accounted for more than 75 per cent of Cuba's exports and the employment of a half million sugar workers for the short period of three or four months out of the year.

To realize the importance of sugar in Cuba's economy it should be remembered that two-thirds of the national income stems directly or indirectly from sugar. Before nationalization in the autumn of 1960, the sugar industry represented an investment of $650 million, of which the United States shared in some $300 million. Of Cuba's 161 sugar mills 30 were controlled by a dozen or so United States interests, which accounted for 37 per cent of the island's production. In 1939 American enterprises produced 55 per cent of the crop, the Cuban 22 per cent. By the 1950's the proportion was reversed—62 per cent of the crop was produced by the Cubans, 36 per cent by the Americans.

Another negative aspect of Cuba's prerevolutionary economy was its chronic condition of semistagnation. The rate of economic growth—close to 1½ per cent—was one of the lowest in the world. Unemployment, that old enemy of the working class and friend of communism, was a permanent source of frustration for hundreds of thousands of boys and girls who each year reached the working age. As far as these young people were concerned, Cuba's old economic order had little to offer them but unemployment or a low-paid government position. To them, both Fidelism and communism had great appeal, but especially the former because of its nationalistic and patriotic fervor. Thousands and thousands of these young men and women are now in the People's Militia, Fidel Castro's most important military force.

Cuba's one-crop sugar economy—responsible for the chronic unemployment that Fidel tried to solve through agricultural diversification, land reform, and industrialization—was almost entirely dependent on the United States.

Since the establishment of the republic in 1902, Cuba sold at least 70 per cent of its exports of sugar, tobacco, and other products to the United States. During all those years Cuba has, in return, purchased from the United States about 80 per cent of its machinery, chemicals, new materials, and thousands of other items required by a nation which has never been able to produce even its own food.

From the time Fidel Castro marched into Havana in January, 1959, following the fall of the Batista regime, the bearded young revolutionary leader—*Lider Máximo* (maximum leader), as Fidel prefers to be called—he has repeatedly said that he would make Cuba "economically and politically independent of the United States." Unhappily he has accomplished it—not by creating an economically independent nation but by making it a nation entirely dependent on the Soviet Union and the communist bloc.]

In the autumn of 1959 it became clear to a growing number of Castro's assistants, including Dr. Felipe Pazos, internationally respected top Cuban economist, that Fidel Castro's policy had no other aim than that of establishing conditions favorable to a rapid communization of Cuba.

During the first six months of the Cuban revolutionary regime Castro had not only the admiration of the world but the absolute loyalty of Cubans of every class. Even landowners recognized the distortions in the country's economy and the need for reforms. All Cubans, including those affected by the sweeping reforms, approved Fidel Castro's efforts to rid the country of chronic unemployment through agricultural diversification and giving land to the landless. Castro used to say that after giving the land to the landless he would then make available low-cost loans, equipment, technical assistance, marketing service, so that the peasants would become prosperous small farmers. They would thus—according to Fidel's plan—be able to buy all sorts of goods that heretofore had been imported from the United States but would now be manufactured by industries newly created in Cuba. In the creation of these new industries both domestic and foreign private capital was welcomed by the revolutionary government. During his United States tour in the spring of 1959 Castro denied any plans for the expropriation of private property and called for foreign private capital investment in Cuba for the industrialization of the country.

It is interesting to recall that during the first part of his regime many of the wealthy people in Cuba were ready to make personal sacrifices to help accomplish the reforms; many offered their advice, personal service, and even their money; others were ready to make any investment in accordance with the government's new economic trends.

Castro was not at all interested. He not only avoided people of wealth and prominence but refused to make use of men with wide experience in business. He would have no one in his official family except his barbudos or those who had demonstrated an unfailing loyalty to the revolution and to himself. From the very beginning his devotion was to the masses, and he felt at ease only when he was among his guajiros (farm hands).

Since the advent of the Castro regime on January 1, 1959, Cuba has experienced far-reaching social and economic changes. During the first year and a half those structural changes were carried out under a semicapitalist economic system and apparently were not aimed at an over-all change in the social structure of the Cuban society. Apart from nationalization, the most striking change in Cuba during this period was the large shift in income to wage earners. This was brought about by a rise of 20 per cent in wages. The large increase in income of workers led to a corresponding increase in their consumption, despite a reduction in total imports. Although wages had risen, businessmen did not raise prices for fear of being considered counterrevolutionary, and in the hope of escaping nationalization they maintained production.

The Cuban government officially labeled 1959 "The Year of Liberation," but the economists should call it "The Year of Consumption." In 1959 there was a shift of more than $250 million from private investment to private and government consumption. Although there was a large volume of government investment, it was scattered among many small projects, most of them of a welfare character. Even investment was mainly oriented to immediate increases in consumption (beaches, parks, low-cost housing, schools, etc.). The year 1959 was a boom year for Cuba and what is more important, it was for the first time a boom not based on a world market demand for sugar. It occurred in spite of a sharp drop in private construction, which traditionally has been one of the main economic activities of the country. The picture in 1960 and the first half of 1961 is completely different. This period could be called "the transition period," from the capitalist system to socialism or communism. This has been carried out at a faster tempo than in the so-called people's republics of Eastern Europe.

Given the fast tempo at which the Cuban economy is being socialized and the large proportion of producing capacity that has already passed from private to government management, one essential question in the Cuban situation is the effect on production of this rapid and widespread change in ownership and management. Ordinarily the fast pace of socialization would be expected to bring about a fall in production in both the socialized and the still-private enterprises—in the former because of the inexperience of the new managers and in the latter because of the inhibiting effects of impending expropriation. Production has not fallen, as a rule, in socialized farms and industries, in spite of the inexperience of the new managers. The printing press has put vast sums at the disposal of the socialized enterprises, bookkeeping has been set aside as a counterrevolutionary hindrance, and inefficiency has only resulted in highly increased costs, rather than in decreased production.

By the summer of 1961 the process of socialization had been completed. Cuba is in word and deed a socialist republic, just as any of those that compose the Soviet Union.

Cuba should already be considered a socialist society; the upper classes have been destroyed and the middle class has been uprooted.

Opposition to communism has appeared in all classes, including the peasantry. The guajiro had been promised his own plot of land; instead, with relatively few exceptions, he finds himself working for a collective or a state farm, and consequently he feels cheated. It should be stressed that many of the anti-Castro freedom fighters in the Escambray Mountains and Oriente Province were peasants.

The core of the opposition to the communist regime is among the teachers, students, writers, doctors, lawyers, engineers, priests, storekeepers, office workers, in general, the white-collar class—the same class that fought Batista's dictatorship and contributed to Castro's victory.

It is certain that these people would not have given their support to Fidel if they had had the slightest indication of what was going to happen under him.

Fidel Castro could not have won without the support of this class of Cubans; the guerrilla warfare waged by him in the mountains would never have brought about the defeat of the Batista regime. He succeeded only because thousands of civilians behind the lines supported him. It was precisely the kind of promises Castro made to the Cuban people that enabled him to get their overwhelming support, and the record shows that these promises were neither socialist nor communist.

As early as September, 1953, during the Moncada trial, Fidel Castro promised, as before stated, that the first revolutionary law would proclaim the Constitution of 1940 as "the supreme law of the land." In this and in subsequent statements Castro promised "absolute guarantee of freedom of information of newspaper and radio, and of all the individual and political rights guaranteed by the Constitution." He also promised, upon the overthrow of Batista, a provisional government that within a year would call for a general and unfettered election.

In the summer of 1957, following meetings held in the Sierra Maestra with Dr. Felipe Pazos and Raúl Chibás,[4] Castro came out with his first political declaration from the Sierra Maestra, which contained a previous promise of a general election at the end of one year and an absolute guarantee of freedom of information, press, and of all individual and political rights guaranteed by the 1940 Cuban Constitution.

At the end of the same year (December 14, 1957), in a letter addressed to the Cuban Liberation Council in Miami, Fidel Castro said that the "prime duty" of a post-Batista provisional government should be the celebration of general elections within a year and the right of all political parties and groups, even during the tenure of the provisional government, to put forward programs, organize themselves, and participate in a general election under the provisions of the 1940 Constitution and the Electoral Code of 1943.[5] It should be noted too that in an article in *Coronet* magazine of February, 1958, Castro wrote of fighting for a "genuine representative government," "truly honest" general elections within twelve months, "full and untrammeled" freedom of public information and all communication media, and the establishment of all personal and political rights set forth in

[4] Raúl Chibás, who is now one of the leaders of the anti-Castro MRP (People's Revolutionary Movement), is a brother of the late Senator Eduardo Chibás, who had been a candidate for the presidency and was famous for his fight against corruption and graft in high places.

[5] The Electoral Code of 1943 was widely considered by Cubans to be a most efficient instrument for keeping elections honest.

the Cuban Constitution of 1940. It is worth pointing out that in that article Castro defended himself against charges made by some anti-Batista Cubans that he was "plotting to replace a military dictatorship with a revolutionary dictatorship."

In the same *Coronet* article Castro said that he favored a land reform to benefit the landless peasant, and he clearly stated that the peasant would be given title to the land. He further stated that just compensation for such expropriation would be made to the owners. Just as important, however, in the same article Castro said that he had no plans for expropriation or for nationalizing foreign investments in Cuba, and that he had changed earlier ideas to extend government ownership to public utilities. It will be recalled that in his Moncada trial speech Castro suggested that public utilities should be operated by the government.

On the nationalization issue Castro wrote in the same article:

I personally have come to feel that nationalization is, at best, a cumbersome instrument. It does not seem to make the state any stronger, yet it enfeebles private enterprise. Even more importantly, any attempt at wholesale nationalization would obviously hamper the principal point of our economic platform—industrialization at the fastest possible rate. For this purpose, foreign investments will always be welcome and secure here.

Time and again Castro repeated that his goals were political freedom, free elections, and social justice. In May, 1958, he told Jules Dubois, top Latin-American correspondent for the Chicago *Tribune* and author of the book *Fidel Castro*, that never had the 26th of July Movement talked about socializing or nationalizing industries, adding that all the gossip was "simply stupid fear of our revolution." In short, Castro promised a free and democratic Cuba dedicated to social justice and economic growth of the country's wealth in order to ensure stable employment to the majority of the people.

Such were the promises Castro made to the Cuban people. It was to assure these goals that the rebel army maintained itself in the hills, that the Cuban people turned against Batista, and that all elements of the revolution in the end supported the 26th of July Movement. Because of all this, Castro had the wholehearted support of the people when Batista fled.

Another contributing factor was the faith of the Cuban people in his promise to give Cuba an honest government. The Cuban people did not want Batista nor the kind of representative government symbolized by the administrations of Prío and Grau. They did want a government that would forever end corruption in government and that would correct some of the main failures of the Cuban economic system—chronic unemployment, economic stagnation, and an economy dependent on the fluctuation of a single crop.

A revolution was indeed a necessary step in Cuba given the fact that there was no other alternative to rid the country of the Batista dictatorship. From the time of Batista's seizure of power in 1952 various efforts were made to find a peaceful solution to the situation created by the military coup, but without success, for the results of these efforts always narrowed down to the need for holding honest elections.

The elections held by Batista in the fall of 1958 were not accepted by the Cuban people in general, and they were held in a situation of tension and civil war throughout the island. The revolutionary change was the only way to bring back constitutional government to Cuba. Shortly after these rigged elections, which resulted in Batista's candidate, Dr. Andrés

Rivero Agüero, being elected, the Cuban Army made several attempts to unseat Batista.

Another evidence that Batista's rigged elections were no solution was the effort made by former Ambassador William D. Pawley to get Batista to resign. On December 9, 1958, Pawley flew to Havana secretly to try to persuade his old friend of thirty years' standing to step out and let a "caretaker" junta take over, which would be both anti-Castro and anti-Batista.

On December 17, the American ambassador in Havana, Mr. Earl E. T. Smith, on instructions of the State Department, told Batista that "the United States, or rather certain influential people in the United States, believed that he could no longer maintain effective control in Cuba, and that they believed it would avoid a great deal of further bloodshed if he were to retire." [6]

This brings us back again to the question of the need for a revolution in Cuba to put an end to the corrupt and brutal dictatorship of General Fulgencio Batista. But what kind of revolution? There are indeed different kinds of revolutions. The bolshevik revolution in Russia in 1917 was not the same as the French Revolution in 1789 or the American Revolution in 1776; and the revolutionary wars for independence in South America were not the same as the Revolutionary War of the United States.

Cuba verily needed a revolution or a military coup to overthrow the Batista regime. According to the most conservative anti-Batista Cuban leaders, the country needed only the re-establishment of constitutional government and the end of corruption and graft. In the opinion of this group

[6] Senate Internal Security Subcommittee, *Communist Threat to the United States through the Caribbean*, Part 9 (Aug. 27, 30, 1960), p. 687.

economic and social reforms were not needed, for they believed that Cuba was already becoming less of an export economy and that she was already on the road toward industrialization through foreign capital investment, which would gradually solve the problem of chronic unemployment.

On the other hand, there were the radicals who thought Cuba needed deep economic and social changes in order to find a solution to the problem of unemployment and a colonial economy based on a one-crop system. This radical group was also in favor of a sweeping reform in the land-tenure system of Cuba, a country where nine out of ten rural homes (bohíos) [7] of the guajiros have only kerosene lamps and less than 3 per cent have water piped into their homes. But no one, even the radicals, visualized a totalitarian soviet-type solution for the land problem and for the improvement of the lowest strata of the Cuban population.

There were of course a few Communists who were attracted by the "wonderful achievements" of communist totalitarian economies. But the truth is that, prior to the triumph of Fidel Castro, practically no one in Cuba ever thought or spoke of the need for a communist, statist or, more discreetly, "socialist" economy to promote the economic development of Cuba.

---

[7] The bohíos cannot be compared with the peasant homes of Europe. They are actually huts with dirt floors and roofs thatched with dried palms.

CHAPTER V

The Challenge of Castroism

LAND reform logically constituted the backbone of a revolution carried out in a country such as Cuba where agriculture is indeed the chief industry, producing food for domestic consumption, items for export to foreign countries, raw materials for Cuban industry, and serving as a major source of employment for most of the island's population.

Before the agrarian reform most of Cuba's farms (particularly large farms or large landholdings) specialized in one item—cattle, sugar, tobacco, or coffee—the last three items almost entirely for export. Cuba's largest and most important crop was sugar. In recent years successful efforts had been made to increase other crops for export and to expand rice cultivation, hog breeding, and dairy farming to meet the demands of the steadily growing population. Nevertheless, Cuba remained a country that imported many of its foodstuffs. Its economy depended upon the export market for its sugar, which accounted for more than three-fourths of the total value of its exports. And, although Cuba also exported such items as tobacco, pineapples, winter vegetables, and had recently stepped up its export of coffee, it was still far from freeing its economy from dependence on sugar.

On the other hand, the land-tenure system of prerevolutionary Cuba spelled unchanging poverty for great masses of landless peasants. According to the 1946 Cuban Agricultural Census, more than one-third of all the crop land in Cuba was owned by about 900 large corporations, some of them possessing as much as 610,000 acres. Small farmers working 25 acres or less had only a tenth as much land as was given over to the latifundias (big landholdings), and this was generally the poorest land. It is a well-known fact that the big sugar companies and the cattle ranches owned about 70 million acres of land, and practically dominated Cuban agriculture. Sugar latifundias took up 22 per cent of the total land area of Oriente Province, 27 per cent of Camagüey, and 36 per cent of Matanzas; the whole of the Isle of Pines, 3,000 square kilometers, was owned by four landlords.

However, the bulk of Cuba's farm land was owned by sugar planters (colonos), who controlled more than 75 per cent of the cultivated land dedicated to sugar. One third of the colonos owned holdings not exceeding 33 acres of cultivated land, while the rest owned holdings ranging from 33 to 88 acres. The colonos are usually well-to-do farmers. They generally had agreements with the sugar mills for the sale of the sugar cane produced on their lands for export and domestic consumption. Aside from the colonos, there were families who rented their land from large estates or from prosperous colonos. In many cases, the rental agreements were made several decades ago when fees for land rentals were comparatively low.

There also existed in Cuba a significant number of sharecroppers, whose well-being depended upon the moral scruples of individual landowners and the various hazards of farming—time, place, weather, etc. However, the greater part of the Cuban rural population was composed of the guajiros, who possessed neither land nor permanent shelter and were hired to perform manual labor on the plantations and farms owned by the big processing companies or by the colonos.

Before social legislation was enacted by the Cuban Congress after the 1933 revolution, the guajiros labored in the fields up to 14 and 16 hours a day, six days a week; they were underpaid and very nearly always remained poor and without possessions. Historically this large group of needy, landless farm laborers had created great pressure in Cuba for social change. Before the thirties they were terrorized by the Rural Guard, a segment of the former Cuban Army, whose duty it was to keep order in the countryside. Years ago it could be said that the Rural Guard was the "army of the latifundistas" (big landowners).

It is indisputable that the Agrarian Reform Act which Fidel signed at his old headquarters at La Plata in the Sierra Maestra, on May 17, 1959, was the turning point in the transformation of the social structure of Cuba. Up to then the Castro government had limited itself to launching minor reforms which did not change the basic structure of Cuban society. The real change was indeed the epochal land reform and the replacement of the latifundia.

With the enactment of the Cuban Agrarian Reform Law the transformation of the economic and social structure of Cuban society began. The provisions of the act were, on the surface, moderate. Private landowners were permitted to keep 990 acres of land, and up to 3,300 acres in land devoted to the raising of sugar, rice, or cattle. Larger estates were to be expropriated, leaving the owner with a nucleus of 990 acres, payment for which would be made with 20-year 4½ per cent bonds based on the tax value of the property made by the owners themselves. There were strong objections to this provision of the law, as this land had been appraised for taxes at far less than its actual value, for obvious reasons of course.

Another characteristic of the law is the provision prohibiting any private enterprise owning Cuban land unless all the stockholders are Cuban. Henceforth, no foreigners may buy or inherit Cuban land according to the Agrarian Reform Act. One of the most important features of this law was the creation of the National Institute for Agrarian Reform (INRA), which is "an autonomous entity with its own juridical personality for the purpose of applying and enforcing this law."

The INRA (which has been criticized as a state within a state) is, from the legal standpoint, a government corporation similar to the Tennessee Valley Authority of the United States, but actually it had very different purposes. Until recently INRA was the most powerful weapon in the hands of the revolutionary government in carrying out the collectivization of Cuban agriculture and setting up the basis for the industrial development of the country along Marxist lines. The INRA has an industrial division, but since the spring of 1961 the industrialization of the country has been taken out of its jurisdiction and placed under the newly created Ministry of Industries, headed by Che Guevara.

One of the main purposes of the INRA was to promote agrarian cooperatives. Article 43 of the Agrarian Reform Law states:

Whenever possible INRA will promote agrarian cooperatives. The agrarian cooperatives organized by INRA on lands available to it under the provisions of this Law shall be under its direction, and it shall reserve the right to appoint the managers thereof for the purpose of ensuring their better development during the initial stage of this type of economic and social organization and until greater autonomy is granted it by law.

It should be stressed that INRA was given power not only to establish cooperatives but also to direct their establishment "whenever possible." Thus from the very inception of the agrarian reform, Castro and his associates had in mind the collectivization of Cuban agriculture. All cooperatives had been organized by INRA and operated by INRA officials.

While it is obviously true that the general trend of Castro's agricultural reform appears to be toward complete socialization of Cuba's agriculture through the establishment of INRA cooperatives of both the Chinese commune and the Soviet Union state farm type (sovkhoz), it is just as true that with this agrarian reform a new class of private farmers has emerged in Cuba, most of whom once worked on someone else's land as planters, leasers, sharecroppers, or just squatters. These people are individualists with a strong sense of possessing private property.

To all these new farmers INRA has given aid "Vital Minimum" (V.M.) of 66 acres of land with the right to buy an additional 99 acres. According to Captain Antonio Núñez Jiménez, director of INRA, 21,425 titles of property have been given to the mentioned group of landless peasants. According to the Agrarian Reform Act, these titles are given under the following conditions:

The amount of the land is set by the law as sixty-seven and two-thirds acres. The land may never be mortgaged or sold. Only one child can inherit it; the holders must accept the administration of the institute, plant the crops ordered and deliver the production to the institute, accepting the prices set by the government.

Recently, however, INRA has abolished the policy of making landowners of the peasants and now only on rare occasions are titles issued to individual farmers. Since the beginning of 1961 the only property titles issued have been to sugar cane planters or colonos who had actually held the land for the past twenty-five years.

It is a widely held view that Castro has always had in mind the socialization of Cuban agriculture but that he felt it would be better in the early phases of the reform to give the land outright to the peasant farmer, for to have herded them into cooperatives would have conflicted with the habits of these small holders of working the land. According to some of his intimates, Castro avoided making the early Russian mistake of stubbornly insisting on complete socialization and abolition of private property from the very beginning. Following the division of the land in Soviet Russia there emerged a class called the kulaks who were opposed to going into the collective farms and the state farms. When Stalin decided to socialize Russian agriculture the kulaks were wiped out.

Fidel's way was indeed more humane, for by leading the landless peasants into believing that he intended to make them owners of parcels of land he won for himself and for the revolution an important segment of the rural population of Cuba. A provision of the Agrarian Reform Law canceled all leases held by tenant farmers, including sharecropper agreements. But it should be pointed out that of more than 150,000 tenant farmers only 21,425, or about 15 per cent, of them received titles of property. The remainder have been "persuaded" to go into INRA's cooperatives which, in the beginning of the agrarian reform, were established to produce crops that could best be grown in large undivided areas, e.g., cattle, sugar, and rice.

At present there are 625 cooperatives, most of them in cane, with 122,448 members organized on the lands of the 161 sugar mills that were nationalized in 1960. The Cuban cooperative is not made up of the pooling of individual peasant holdings as in the kolkhoz (collective farm) which is actually an autonomous enterprise owning its land and capital, electing its own management, and determining its policy within the framework of a general economic plan. There is nothing similar to this in the Cuban cooperative. The land belongs to INRA, the management is appointed by INRA, and the workers are paid wages. It might be said that they are more like the state farms of the Soviet Union and the Chinese communes.

Most of the Cuban cooperatives are nowadays the so-called people's farms (granjas del pueblo), which are organizationally identical to the state farm of the Soviet Union. The land and the capital belong to INRA, which also takes the profits, if any. The state farm is just a big latifundium run by the government and, as before, the manual labor is done by the peasant, who receives certain benefits—free housing, free medical and dental care, and free education.

The construction of modern dwellings for the cooperativista is the first step taken by INRA when organizing a cooperative. Most of these dwellings are comfortable structures of cement block with roofs of processed bagasse [1] and have tile floors, electricity, running water, toilets, etc. Some of the cooperatives have prefabricated houses.

Free medical and dental care is provided to the cooperativista by INRA. Practically all cooperatives have a school and small clinic served by a physician. In 1960 Fidel Castro made a television appeal to young doctors to serve voluntarily

[1] Bagasse is the crushed cane left after the sugar is extracted.

throughout the countryside for six months, and many graduates of the Medical School of Havana University responded. It is now compulsory for all medical students to serve for a period of six months in the remote regions of Cuba before they can be graduated. The Cuban government is now waging a big health campaign and one of its main goals is the checking of parasitic and other diseases in the areas that have never known until now either doctor or hospital. This same policy is being carried out in the field of education, and young teachers must serve in the most remote sections of the island.

In Batista's time there were 5,600 rural schools and 12,000 urban schools; in 1961, according to the Ministry of Education, the figures are 13,000 and 19,000, respectively. This year, 1961, is being called "The Year of Education" as a major push has started, in which the government plans to eliminate a 35 per cent illiteracy by the end of the year. Although it is being called The Year of Education, the director of INRA, Captain Antonio Núñez Jiménez, recently stated that 1961 will also be known as "El año del Paredón" (The Year of the Firing Squad), as Castro has stated his intention to put an end to all attempts to overthrow his regime, by strong-arm methods and summary executions.

Another advantage of the cooperative system has been the crop diversification by those enterprises dedicated to the large-scale production of commodities like sugar, tobacco, rice, and other major products. In all these cooperatives the management compels the production on a small scale of new products, such as potatoes, beans, vegetables, tropical fruits, etc., which are marketed through the people's stores (tienda del pueblo), another innovation in socialist Cuba. These people's stores, which have been established in every cooperative, are in no way like the old company store. They are a nonprofit state organization which gives the cooperative the benefit of lower prices. They are well stocked, as in Cuba today all imports, exports, and distribution are under government control, and have priority over privately owned stores, which actually have gone into bankruptcy all over the countryside. There are relatively few people's stores in the cities, and there private enterprise still operates. In Havana itself there are no so-called stores of the people, but the government has nationalized all the big chain grocery stores, which it now operates.

Castro has proceeded to the socialization of Cuba at a tempo faster than that of the Russian Revolution. Within two years of proclaiming the Agrarian Reform Castro has achieved the complete destruction of the petite bourgeoisie as an economic class through the Agrarian Reform and the nationalization of all phases of production, even small enterprises. In the agricultural field the socialization is complete, according to Iron Curtain experts. Castro has skipped one stage toward socialization which has been carried in all communist countries. Well-known Marxist economists and propagandists have generally agreed that the approach to collectivized agriculture in underdeveloped countries would have to be indirect: first the distribution of land to peasants, later the introduction of cooperatives in which the farmer would not lose ownership of the land, followed by the more or less rapid evolution toward collective property through both the kolkhoz and sovkhoz systems. Even in Red China the communes did not come at once. Mao Tse-tung first divided the cultivated land among the peasants on an individual basis and it was not until much later in 1957 that he decided to take the big leap toward the communes, which are heavily militarized cooperatives of peasants and rural workers aimed at agricultural and industrial development of the region. Castro has not gone so far as militarization of the cooperatives, but he has bypassed that stage of distribution of land to the landless, except for the small percentage mentioned previously whose ownership of the land is limited.

The Russian Bolsheviks also distributed land to millions of small farmers, and it was not until much later that they decided to establish the system of collective and state farms. Castro's agrarian reform was apparently aimed at the establishment of a dual system of private and collective farms, but after the first few months he decided that the best way to the fast socialization of agriculture was through the collective system of the state farm, which he said is the best means of providing free education to, and indoctrination of, thousands of young children.

One of the new features of Castro's agrarian reform is the so-called youth farm, a 167-acre colony planned for children from ten years of age and upward. These youth farms are part of the people's farm system in which adults are taught modern agricultural methods. On each of the people's farms 167 acres are utilized for a youth farm. The children will be fed, housed, and go to school on the farm under revolutionary discipline, which means communist discipline. It is worth mentioning here that in early 1961 Fidel Castro announced that a thousand youths will come from the Soviet Union to Cuba to work on the farms and a thousand Cuban youths will be sent to the agricultural cooperatives of the Soviet Union to learn their methods.

The thousands of cooperativistas do not object to the intensive indoctrination of their children that is going on throughout the whole of Cuba. The middle class and the more responsible people from the villages and the cities are horrified at Castro's plans to communize the youth of Cuba. The only thing the poor ignorant peasant objects to is the communist discipline for himself and the drastic reductions in his wages, especially those in the sugar industry, which are now 40 per cent less than before nationalization of the Cuban industry. They do not have the right to strike or complain, or to change jobs.

The main objective of the Agrarian Reform Law was to diversify agriculture in order to make Cuba less dependent on a one-crop economy and at the same time to establish a sound rural population that would create a potential market for the industrialization of the country. There is no doubt that agrarian reform has, to a certain degree, achieved some of those aims. New crops, such as cotton, have been produced in Cuba and new lands have been brought under cultivation in corn, rice, tomatoes, beans, and all kinds of vegetables, many of which had to be imported previously. According to INRA's figures, production levels in a wide range of crops have jumped dramatically. In the latest meeting of the Economic Commission for Latin America (ECLA), which was held in May of 1961 in Santiago de Chile, the Cuban Minister of Finance, Lieutenant Commander Rolando Díaz Aztarain, stated that the Cuban Agrarian Reform "is the only one in the world that has brought about an immediate increase of production levels." He also said that cane production has increased 25 per cent over the last crop harvested in the last year of Batista and added that it has reached the highest level of production in Cuba's history. The 1960 rice crop was 30 per cent over the crop of 1958, and he expects that the rice production of this year, 1961, will increase another 25 per cent. Regarding corn, Díaz Aztarain said that its production has increased 50 per cent over the 1958 level. He also gave percentages of production increases on many other agricultural products and called the attention of the other ECLA delegates to the fact that Cuba is now producing cotton in great quantities. By 1965, he claimed, Cuban cotton production will be able to meet the textile needs of the country. He stated that, with the exception of meat and cattle raising, the production of every commodity has increased.

Despite the glowing picture painted by Díaz Aztarain in the ECLA meeting, the truth is that in Cuba today there is a growing shortage of food: meat, milk, butter, eggs, chickens, beans, vegetables, and fruits. "No hay" (there is none) is the most frequently heard phrase in all commercial establishments in Cuba. Former President Dr. Ramón Grau San Martín, in a recent discussion of the Cuban situation with an American correspondent, said: "General No Hay is the one who is going to defeat the Reds."

The meat shortage is so acute that for the first time in Cuban history it has been rationed. But this shortage did not come as a surprise to well-informed Cubans. When I fled Cuba in 1960 it was generally accepted—even by Cubans still enthusiastic about the Castro regime—that the livestock industry, one of the greatest sources of Cuba's national wealth, had been destroyed by INRA to the extent that Cuba was importing cattle. The destruction of this important industry was the result of the ignorance of many INRA officials, who, in the early days of the agrarian reform, began shipping the best breeding cattle from the confiscated ranches to the slaughterhouses. This did not prevent the handsome magazine published by INRA from showing a picture of a six-year-old bull as an example of success in livestock breeding, although the agrarian reform was only a year old. In all prob-

ability some of the fine INRA specimens were from some of
the largest confiscated United States ranches in Cuba, such
as those owned by Sumner Pingree of Massachusetts, or from
the Becerra Cattle Company, owned jointly by King Ranch
and the Manati Sugar Company.

Fidel himself has had to admit publicly that there is a
shortage of food and that the attempt of his government to
feed the island from locally grown products has not been too
successful. He conceded that only the United States can supply the foods the island needs and added that the socialist
countries have their economies planned according to their
own needs and have not the surpluses of food Cuba wants.

Despite this, Castro is trying to overcome this shortage by
increasing imports from the Soviet bloc. In most of Cuba's
grocery stores may be found rice from China, canned lobster
and beef from the Soviet Union at high prices, and straw-
berry jam and hams from Poland, but they do not suffice to
meet the needs of the Cuban people, who, for the first time
in Cuban history, have to form queues outside the stores. In
addition, agricultural experts from the communist countries
are working with Castro officials to speed up production and
to correct much of the mismanagement in both cooperative
and distributive systems.

The food shortage has been a factor in the worsening of an
uncontrolled inflation, which the Castro government tackled
with one of its characteristic harsh measures—the compulsory
exchange of all paper money for a new currency. On August
4 the Cuban government announced that all paper money
would be void after midnight of August 6, and seventy-two
hours were allowed for the turning in of old currency for new
bills. According to the new law, each person could appear
only once at the exchange center. In exchange for his old

bills he received 200 of the new pesos in cash; anything over that was placed in a special account set up by the government in the National Bank, from which he could not draw anything for one week. He was forced to take an oath as to his identity, residence, the persons he represented, and the ownership of the bills he presented. A false oath made him subject to imprisonment, plus confiscation of all his assets.

The reason given by the Castro government for this measure was that it would remove the inflationary pressure of "hundreds of millions of pesos" held abroad by anti-Castro Cubans, who sent them into Cuba clandestinely to finance the underground. An editorial in one of Castro's newspapers remarked with satisfaction that "if the counterrevolutionaries want to continue their intrigues they will have to use Yankee dollars to finance them."

The effect of this measure has been felt more sharply by Cubans in Cuba—including, but not limited to, the underground—than by the refugees and foreigners at whom it was ostensibly directed. It has been a tragedy to thousands of middle-class Cubans, who, in fear of confiscation of bank accounts, have kept at least part of their savings in socks, boxes, mattresses, or even buried in the ground. And for all these who have not turned in their savings for fear of being questioned this new measure means starvation. Many of them are the outcasts of the new communist society and have no means of income.

On the other hand, this highly unpopular measure fits the government's need to combat inflation, which has worsened with a sharply expanded abundance of currency chasing after the scarce consumer goods. In any case, the Castro government has now the means to achieve any degree of savings that it wishes. But in human terms the currency exchange was another painful experience for many Cubans in the class-less society emerging on the island.

Despite all these grim facts of life in the new police state that is Cuba, there is no doubt that Castro's revolution is aimed at raising many people out of inhuman squalor and bringing to them some hope of a decent life. In less than three years the Castro government has accomplished many good things for the underdog. It has tried to put an end to gambling and prostitution, which made Havana notorious in all the Americas. While it is true that it has destroyed the upper classes and the once revolutionary-minded middle class and has forced the professional class to seek asylum in the United States and other neighbor countries, it is also a fact that it has tried to improve the living standards of the peasant and the unskilled worker, bringing to them not only welfare benefits but that intangible essential element of prideful participation in the present and hope for the future which is the keynote to the progress and self-respect of the human being. These were the humanitarian goals of the Cuban revolution that gave Castro such immense popularity in Cuba and in the Latin-American countries.

I have seen many of these achievements of the Cuban revolution myself. I have visited public beaches on the north and south coasts of the island—even in remote places like Playa Girón, which was one of the beaches where the anti-Castro Cuban Liberation Army landed in Bahía de Cochinos. These are lovely spots with restaurants, sleeping accommodations, playgrounds for children, in places which were formerly private property and closed to the people. Before taking over the luxurious, aristocratic clubs in Havana and other places in the island, Castro had built public beaches for the people which had all modern facilities, and some of those beaches were often better than many of the private clubs in Havana. I have also seen tourist centers in the mountains built for the people on beautiful sites, new workers' quarters alongside the old hovels where for decades families lived packed together, without water, without gas, without electricity.

All these accomplishments have made in the minds of the people a sort of cult of Fidel, who is still regarded by many uneducated people as a god. Even the communist indications in Castro's regime have not diminished his popularity among the illiterate masses.

I remember a day in the country where some people were dancing in one of the new tourist centers, and chanting:

> If Fidel is a Communist
> Put me on the list also,
> Because if he is one,
> Then I am one too.

Not all the humble people, as Fidel calls the peasants and unskilled workers, are happy with the new totalitarian regime. Once in a small village in central Cuba I met a friend who owned a small farm which had not been affected by the agrarian reform. He told me that not all landless peasants were happy with the cooperative system. Many of them think they have been cheated as they have not received property titles to lands that were offered to them, and they are now forced to work in cooperatives where half their salary is paid in scrip which entitles them to buy only in the people's store of the cooperative. There has also been a general decrease in salaries paid by cooperatives. These reductions are mainly in the form of "voluntary" contributions forced on them by INRA officials or some of Fidel's drives. Every wage earner

in Cuba must contribute 4 per cent of his salary for industrialization and 3 per cent for arms and planes.

Many persons also have begun to realize that a new system of inhuman exploitation has been established—the Secret
Police is everywhere and everyone is in fear of it. An increasing rhythm of terror is spreading all over the countryside and
any complaints about conditions could mean arrest and a
sentence to hard labor.

Service in the militia is practically compulsory for every
peasant and military discipline governs his life, even in his
free time, when he is "persuaded" to attend a lecture on
agrarian reform or on Marxism. The easygoing, carefree
Cuban rejects the military discipline of the militia, which is
now commanded by communist fanatics. If there is discontent among the members of the cooperatives for the many
reasons mentioned, there is much greater discontent among
the laborers who have now been forced to make sacrifices for
the industrialization of the country.

Second in importance to the Agrarian Reform has been
industrialization. The economic program of the 26th of July
Movement, drawn up by Felipe Pazos and Regino Boti, while
Castro was still in the mountains struggling against Batista,
called for Cuba's industrialization through both private and
public capital investment. From the very beginning of the
revolution Castro and his cohorts have advocated industrialization to end chronic unemployment. Nevertheless, practically the only thing that has been done in this direction has
been a great deal of planning by the Central Planning Commission (Junta Central de Planificación, generally referred to
as Juceplan).

In the spring of 1961 a 4-year plan—similar to the Soviet
5-year Gosplan—was announced by Juceplan, intended to

advance Cuba's industrialization along Soviet lines. A significant aspect of the plan is the correlation of Cuba's industrialization with the economy of Soviet Russia and other communist states. This is important because the communist bloc countries supply most of the industrial equipment required.

The announcement of the 4-year plan was accompanied by a reorganization of the government administrative structure, which has been streamlined according to the communist pattern. One of the major shifts has been the creation of the Ministry of Industry, which is headed by Che Guevara, the man responsible for the Soviet bloc orientation of the Cuban government. As has been reported, Guevara moved from the presidency of the National Bank to head this new ministry and will remain economic overlord of the country. Another significant step in the government reorganization is the division of commerce between two ministries—domestic and foreign—as in the Soviet Union. The industrial production goal of Cuba's Juceplan, which is supposed to begin in 1962, was outlined by Guevara a few days before Castro's proclamation of Cuba as a socialist republic on May Day, 1961, as follows:

Steel: An annual production of 500,000 tons. The Soviet Union will set up a plant of 250,000-ton capacity in the Santiago de Cuba area and the old Antillana de Acero plant will be modified to produce 250,000 tons by 1963.

Electricity: Doubled production by the middle of the decade. This will involve building new generating stations with a capacity of 600,000 kilowatts over the next five years. Existing capacity is 920,000 kilowatts.

Cement: Doubled production over the next five years. The present annual rate is almost 1 million tons.

Oil: There were high hopes of finding substantial petroleum deposits. And that Soviet experts had pointed out two probable locations. In addition, Cuba has signed contracts with the Soviet Union for a geological study, the first phase of which is starting. Santiago will get a Soviet-built oil refinery with an annual capacity of 1 million tons.

Textiles: In five years Cuba hopes to achieve self-sufficiency. She is scheduled to receive 200,000 more spindles in the next four years, 150,000 from East Germany and 50,000 from Communist China. Cuba will also receive 3,500 more looms.

Vehicles: Czechoslovakia has agreed to build a plant capable of producing 2,000 tractors, 5,000 trucks, 3,000 motorcycle motors, and 100 stationary motors annually. In addition, Cuba expects to begin producing autos in 1965.

Shipping: A dockyard with complete shipbuilding facilities is to be built by Poland. This will permit the Cubans to produce fishing boats of small tonnage and, later, ships of 10,000-ton capacity for transatlantic trade.

This Juceplan industrialization setup was drafted by a mixed Cuban and Latin-American group, predominantly Communist party members in consultation with a technical group of Iron Curtain experts. This latter group was composed of five Russians, two Czechoslovakians, one Pole, and one East German. It has been reported that Sergei Mikhailovich Kudriatsev, Soviet ambassador in Havana, and Mikhail Kuzmin, Soviet Union vice-minister of foreign trade, who visited Havana in December, 1960, also had a hand in the final plans. So far, however, not a single factory or new industry has been established in Cuba and actually Castro's entire industrial program has been limited to the nationalization of Cuban industry. The Cuban government now owns, or operates a $2.6 billion industrial empire, 43 banks, every apartment in Cuba, 30 insurance companies, the transportation system, mines, fisheries, and 95 per cent of the island's agriculture.

Before Castro Cuba was ranked fifth in Latin America in value of industrial output—trailing Brazil, Argentina, Mexico, and Chile. Manufacturing has been growing steadily in Cuba, although not spectacularly since 1927, when a policy of tariff protection was adopted by the administration of President Machado. By 1958, the last year of Batista's administration, industrial operations were giving employment to almost half a million Cubans, or approximately 19.5 per cent of the labor force.

With the establishment of the National Bank of Cuba in 1950, which provided vitally needed rediscounting and deposit insurance facilities to the country's commercial banks, there began a new era of capitalization and credit facilities. It is safe to say that the National Bank of Cuba under the presidency of Felipe Pazos became the most potent economic force in Cuba; its trained staff of public servants gave the institution a high degree of prestige in government as well as in private circles. It had a particularly effective bank examination department and an outstanding department of economic research. But after Dr. Pazos was replaced by Major Guevara the bank became an instrument of the government to finance agrarian reform and the communization of Cuba. The National Bank is now headed by the former Minister of Commerce, Raúl Cepero Bonilla.

In addition to the National Bank, the administration of President Prío established BANFAIC (Agricultural and Industrial Development Bank). BANFAIC, which was merged into the Industrial Division of INRA in 1960 by Guevara, had

a capital of $26 million, all contributed by the Cuban govern-
ment under President Prío.

The Agricultural Division of the old BANFAIC under Dr.
Justo Carrillo did a remarkable job in promoting rural credit
associations and in improving warehousing and refrigeration
facilities. It played a leading role in the development of rice
production and in financing the mechanization of that industry, as well as many others. It also carried out a series of inves-
tigations and research covering a variety of agricultural and
fishery products.

The work of the Industrial Division of BANFAIC was
equally fruitful. Its most important function—that of promoting new industries—was actively and intelligently carried on.
Aside from direct assistance in the form of loans, it was successful in interesting several foreign concerns to establish
plants in Cuba and carried out a series of market surveys to
determine the possibilities of new industrial undertakings.

It should be noted that BANFAIC concentrated on the
industrial and nonsugar parts of the Cuban economy and this
had partially compensated for the preference of the private
banks for sugar loans. Between 1950 and 1958 loans to the
nonsugar sector of the economy had increased from 28.6 per
cent to 55.6 per cent of total industrial credit. Its largest investment was in the Primera Central Hidroelectrica Cubana,
which built a large dam to harness the hydroelectric power
of the Hanabanilla River, in the province of Las Villas.

In Batista's last administration many new autonomous government credit institutions flourished, the most important of
which were the Economic and Social Development Bank
(Banco de Desarrollo Económico y Social), generally known
as BANDES, the National Finance Corporation of Cuba

(Financiera Nacional de Cuba), and the Cuban Bank for Foreign Trade (Banco Cubano del Comercio Exterior).

All these credit organizations contributed, during Batista's administration, to the expansion of industrial development throughout the island, although in many cases through a corrupted system carried out by politically influential men who asked for government loans which they used to set up private businesses. These private businesses, always protégés of Batista, would put up 10 to 20 per cent of the total capital, the balance being supplied by the Cuban government through BANDES or some of the other new credit institutions.

Despite the revolutionary activities that were going on, the last three years of the Batista regime were marked by great economic development. In 1956, for example, $35.3 million in new capital came to Cuba. That was the year before Castro landed in Oriente Province from Mexico, and in 1958, according to the Bureau of Foreign Commerce of the United States Department of Commerce, new industries valued at more than $15 million started operating in Cuba and new industry requests granted during that year amounted to $42 million, including an $18 million anhydrous ammonia plant and a $7.2 million sulphuric acid plant. In the same year the $24 million Havana Hilton Hotel (Havana Libre since it was taken over by Castro's government in 1960) was built.

An example of the contribution of the new autonomous credit institutions to the economic development of Cuba was the case of the National Finance Corporation of Cuba (Financiera Nacional de Cuba), which participated in the financing of the tunnel built under the harbor of Havana by the French company, Société des Grands Travaux de Marseille, at a cost of $30 million.

If Castro had lived up to his promise to guarantee private investment in Cuba, as he told Jules Dubois of the Chicago *Tribune* in 1958, it is safe to assume that foreign investment would have continued to pour in.

In the early months of the Castro government General Electric was planning to build a lamp factory in Cuba; the Phelps-Dodge Company, with a Dutch partner, was planning to build an $1.8 million copper tube mill and BANFAIC was to furnish half the capital.

Another important project for Cuba was the planned expansion of the Cuban Electric Company (Cia. Cubana de Electricidad), a branch of the American and Foreign Power Company. The Cuban Electric Company, which was nationalized in the fall of 1960, had a plan, initiated during Batista's administration, to invest not less than $147 million in expanding and improving the facilities in Cuba. Of this, about $77 million represented the import content of the total investment, while some $70 million would be spent on Cuban goods and services. Of this, $45.4 million would be spent on power generation, $19.0 million on transmission, $26.4 on replacement, and $42.1 on distribution. Nine new units, representing 282,000 kilowatts of additional capacity, were to be added in the following five years.

In addition, the Cuban Electric Company planned to build an atomic power plant with a 10,000-kw capacity. The contract had already been placed with General Electric Company. Cuba would then have joined the elite of free nations producing atomic power for peaceful purposes. That year, 1958, Cuba and the United States signed an agreement which provided for the supply of uranium for use in a nuclear power plant research project.

Summarizing, Castro has not achieved his aim of industrializing Cuba or of freeing the country from a one-crop economy. Not one new industry has been established. The only thing Guevara has done, besides planning and traveling in the communist countries, has been to integrate along centralized Soviet-type lines all group-related manufacturing plants. He has consolidated 22 companies dealing in vehicles and motors; 13 soft drink companies, including Coca-Cola, now known as Coca-Cola Nacionalizada; 82 shoe manufacturing plants; 9 match factories; 26 plow mills; 10 cleaners and dyers; 27 paper mills; 51 chemical and pharmaceutical plants; 8 salt manufacturers; 34 steel and metal works; 72 cigar and cigarette manufacturers, and 8 communications firms.

Along with the 161 sugar mills, 4 oil refineries, and the principal mines of the country, Guevara has estimated that the Cuban government now owns and operates more than 75 per cent of the industrial production of Cuba.

Concerning Cuba's dependence on sugar, the situation remains the same as before. It is true that Cuba has lost its profitable United States market, which paid a higher price than the world market, but all Cuban sugar is now sold to the Soviet Union and other communist nations, which in turn supply some of the consumer goods which Cuba used to get in the United States. The result has been that the entire Cuban economy is now geared to that of the communist countries and away from the United States. Cuba's entire trade relations are based on barter agreements signed with the Soviet Union, Red China, Czechoslovakia, East Germany, Poland, Hungary, and some neutral countries like Yugoslavia, Indonesia, the then United Arab Republic, and some of the

new nations of Africa like Guinea and Ghana, which, like
Castro's Cuba, are following the communist trend.

In these barter agreements Cuba ships sugar, tobacco, and
other products and in return receives manufactured goods,
and even "complete whole factories." According to Castro
officials, all these agreements have been very "efficient," but
the truth is that not a single machine tool has been received
for the much-publicized new factories which the communist
nations are committed to establish in Cuba.

The shift in Cuba's trade has created many problems,
however. The Soviet Union and the other communist nations
are not supplying all the things that are needed by a country
like Cuba whose entire economy was geared to that of the
United States. A big problem in Cuba today is a shortage in
many supplies and raw materials that used to come at a
day's notice from the United States and now have to travel
halfway around the world and take months to arrive. As a
result of the United States embargo on all exports to Cuba
(except medicines and certain foodstuffs), which was enacted on October 19, 1960, as a counterblow to Castro's
seizure of American-owned property without compensation,
Cuba's transport system is breaking down and industrial output is slowing for lack of replacements. Most of Cuba's machinery and vehicles were made in the United States and
the communist bloc nations cannot furnish the right kinds
of repair parts.

Fortunately for the Castro government, some crucially important items, like catalysts for oil refining, have been supplied by the Soviet Union. In other cases, substitute spare
parts have been produced by the Cubans themselves in their
own machine shops. To meet the rapid rate of depreciation

of automobiles, trucks, and other rolling stock, almost all from the United States, the Cuban government is "cannibalizing" the existing stock and importing new units from Czechoslovakia and other socialist nations from which it will also be possible to obtain spare parts in the future.

As far as agriculture is concerned, Cuba appears to be short of everything. Despite the efforts of the Castro regime to diversify crops and intensify cultivation during its almost three years of power, the Cuban economy still relies entirely upon sugar, the principal crop which was sold partly on the world market but mostly to the United States at 2 or more cents a pound above the world price. Cuba used to sell more than $500 million in goods annually to the United States, mostly sugar, which alone represented more than $350 million, and bought from the United States a corresponding amount of which 25 per cent was in food—lard, rice, wheat, flour, pork, beans, and dairy products.

There is now a radical change in the situation. The Soviet Union is buying most of the Cuban sugar crop. In 1961 the communist bloc bought 4 million tons of sugar at 4 cents per pound, a price slightly higher than the world market. But Russia pays only 20 per cent in cash and the rest in goods. Consequently, Cuba no longer has any dollar exchange worth mentioning. Formerly she had a guaranteed fixed price from her United States quota, and with this income she used to import machinery and all kinds of consumer goods, as well as some food that she was not able to produce in great quantity. While it is true that the Soviet Union has provided Cuba with a $500 million credit to buy machinery, oil, and some consumer goods, as well as some of the island's food needs, including lard and tinned meats, there is no doubt that the

Soviet Union and other communist countries are not in a position to supply in quantity the raw materials and the foods that used to be imported from the United States.

Food is becoming more and more scarce. Meat is rationed and Cuba appears to be short of everything but bread and rice. Drought, lack of skill, organizational difficulties in the newly created cooperatives and state farms, and shortages of seeds, fertilizers and machinery, have resulted in meager crops. Fidel Castro himself has admitted that Cuba's government officials, rather than the United States, must be blamed for the difficulties in increasing and widening Cuba's food production. At a three-day conference in Havana, August 26 to August 28, with 3,500 managers of state farms, cooperatives and factories, Castro said: "We must begin by knowing that we know little and that we lack experience. Those who believe themselves perfect and incapable of making a mistake have no place in our revolution."

Aside from the food situation, the economic problems facing the Cuban revolutionary government are monumental. Not only must the Cuban authorities reorient the island's economy from the United States to communist bloc sources of supply and markets but they are committed to a program of industrial and agricultural expansion. At the same time they must see to it that the collectivization of agriculture and the socialization of commercial and industrial concerns do not drastically lower the level of production.

Despite Cuba's deep economic troubles, Castro is still convinced that with massive Soviet economic aid and austerity at home he will be able to find a socialist solution to Cuba's economic ills—chronic unemployment, one-crop economy, and economic stagnation.

For better or for worse, Castro's communist course has become a point of attraction to many people in Latin America, and the road which will be taken by most other underdeveloped Latin-American countries will be determined in great part by the success or failure of Castro's experiment.

CHAPTER VI

Castro's Impact in Latin America

IT IS AN acknowledged fact that the Cuban revolution has had a tremendous impact in Latin America. There is not a single country in Latin America in which there does not exist considerable sympathy for Castro and his methods. The Cuban revolution has become the inspiration for the majority of the people who want land reform and complete economic and social changes. To them Castro's Cuba is the emblem of the future and the hope for escape from the grinding poverty so prevalent in their countries.

This poverty and desire for change offer a great opportunity to Castro to export his revolution. The intention to do so was made clear by Castro himself when he told a gathering of Latin-American left-wing delegates to the First Latin-American Youth Congress in Havana that his goal was to "turn the Andes into the Sierra Maestra of the American continent."

It was Castro's purpose from the very beginning of his regime to export his revolution throughout the hemisphere. No sooner had he taken over than he began to support the overthrow of governments in the Caribbean area. In the spring and summer of 1959 invasions and attempted invasions of Panama, Nicaragua, the Dominican Republic, and Haiti were made from Cuba.

With the overthrow of the Batista regime, exiles from those countries under dictatorships gathered in Cuba to obtain Castro's support, as he had from the very beginning said that he would support any movement against the remaining dictatorships in the Western Hemisphere. The opponents of the Somoza government, like those of Trujillo's, were divided roughly into two groups—those of a democratic orientation and those of communist sympathies.

I had an opportunity to see and interview many of those exiles while I was a Castro official in the Cuban Foreign Office. I observed that at no time did the noncommunist exiles receive the slightest support from the Cuban government, as the man in charge of the financing of those invasion operations was Che Guevara.

Guevara's attitude disillusioned many of the noncommunist Nicaraguan exiles, who afterward moved into Costa Rica to carry on their operations against the Somoza dynasty on their own and without Cuban support. One of this group was Francisco Ibarra, one of the oldest opponents of the Somoza dictatorship. Guevara bluntly told Ibarra that he would support only a movement that had communist participation. Guevara also dismissed Pedro Joaquín Chamorro, a prominent journalist, publisher and editor of Nicaragua's *La Prensa*, the largest newspaper in Central America.

At the end of May, 1959, Chamorro led a serious attempt to oust Somoza by force. His group invaded Nicaragua from Costa Rica, timing their action to coincide with a general strike within the country which had the support of the employers. However, President Somoza declared martial law and the invaders were defeated by the well-organized and trained Nicaraguan National Guard. The general strike collapsed and this attempt by the noncommunist revolutionary group failed completely.

Meanwhile other Nicaraguan exiled elements coming from Cuba had landed in Honduras near the Nicaraguan border, but were prevented by the Honduras Army from joining the military action. This latter group was communist led and was financed and had the complete support of the Castro government.

The leaders of the procommunist group were Edelberto Torre and Dr. Josefa Palacio, who were supported by Guevara. They had their headquarters in Mexico City and made frequent trips between there and Havana with dollars furnished by the National Bank of Cuba.

Some of the anticommunist Nicaraguan exiles who remained in Cuba were later arrested by the Castro police and charged with being agents of the United States Central Intelligence Agency. One of them, Chester Lacayo, was an important democratic leader. He was arrested with the anticommunist Dominican leader, General Miguel Angel Ramírez, long connected with the Caribbean fight against dictatorships. Ramírez was later released, but Lacayo is still in prison. Lacayo was specifically charged with conspiring with a high official of the United States Department of State to rig false accusations against Castro. Although Castro propaganda accused Lacayo of plotting with the United States government to use Cuba as a base for an invasion against Nicaragua, very few people in Cuba, even Castroites themselves, believed this story. A picture taken of Lacayo leaving the State Department in Washington was shown by Castro in one of his television harangues against the United States.

At the end of June, 1959, the Dominican Republic was

invaded by an expedition organized, trained, and equipped in Cuba with undoubted assistance and knowledge of Cuban officials. The expedition was led by a noncommunist Dominican refugee, Enrique Jiménez, who had served in Castro's army. An officer on active duty in the Cuban armed forces, Major Delio Gómez Ochoa was the second-in-command. During the invasion Gómez Ochoa was captured and held prisoner until recently.

This unsuccessful invasion alerted Washington and other capitals that it would be necessary to call for a meeting of foreign ministers to deal with the turmoil in the Caribbean. The foreign ministers convened in Santiago, Chile, on August 12, 1959. As they met a report was received of another invasion. This time the target was Haiti. The invaders were identified as a group of armed men coming from Cuba under the leadership of a follower of former Haitian Senator Louis Dejoie, a political opponent of President Duvalier. Dejoie was afterward forced to leave Havana permanently. Most of the invaders were either killed or captured by the Haitian Army.

After the Santiago meeting these invasion attempts and armed expeditions were apparently abandoned by the Cuban government, which has seemingly adopted a more subtle means of accomplishing its goal of spreading revolution to other countries.

In close association with Communists and extreme nationalists in the other Latin-American countries, the Cuban diplomats and the correspondents of Castro's news agency Prensa Latina have been organizing, supporting, and encouraging a number of extreme left-wing politicians and movements in other countries to undermine and overthrow if possible the constituted governments. Cuban officials, students, and labor leaders have visited these countries and offered assistance for such revolutionary undertakings. This assistance includes promises of arms for subversive efforts, propaganda material, and most important, training in Cuba in the techniques of guerrilla warfare.

On the eve of the Organization of American States meeting in August, 1960, at San José, Costa Rica, the Department of State notified the Inter-American Peace Committee that the Castro government had established in the Sierra Maestra a training center for communist agents and guerrillas. According to Washington, this was being done through an international work brigade made up of communist personnel from Europe and Asia, including North Korea and Vietnam. This brigade has the support of the Soviet-sponsored World Federation of Democratic Youth. The "brigadiers" were well-trained communist guerrilla fighters who were most likely brought to Cuba to organize the training and political education of Castro's People's Militia as well as the future Latin-American guerrillas who would help "transform the Andes into the Sierra Maestra of the American continent."

The Latin-American Youth Congress hailed the Cuban revolution not only as opening the way to the "liberation" of the other Latin-American republics but also of Puerto Rico. At the opening of the Congress Guevara eulogized a Puerto Rican rebellion movement. He said:

And we wish to greet also one of the delegations that has suffered most perhaps in all America, that of Puerto Rico, which still today ... keeps fighting to take the first step, perhaps the most difficult one, that of achieving at least formally a free government. And we wish the delegates from Puerto Rico to convey my greeting and that of all Cuba to Pedro Albizu Campos; we wish them to carry to Pedro Albizu Campos all our heartfelt cordiality, all our recognition for the road that he has laid out with valor, and all our natural sentiments as free men toward a free man, in spite of his being in a dungeon of the self-styled North American democracy.

At a luncheon given by the government-controlled news agency, Prensa Latina, for the delegates to the Youth Congress the director of the agency, Jorge Masetti, said: "We will continue to announce our presence to our brothers in Puerto Rico and Panama, and we will continue to tell them, 'Plant bombs, throw out the gringos!' "

When the United States broke diplomatic relations with Cuba, about six months later, Castro announced that Cuban citizenship had been conferred on Laura Meneses, wife of Albizu Campos, as well as on Juan Juarbe y Juarbe, head of the Puerto Rican nationalist group in Cuba. Both new "citizens" were appointed members of the Cuban delegation to the United Nations.

From then on there was no doubt of Castro's intentions to export his revolution, not only to the Caribbean area but to the entire Western Hemisphere. In November of that year (1960) the Cuban Embassy in Lima, Peru, was raided by five young anti-Castro Cubans, members of the Cuban Democratic Revolutionary Front. They obtained thousands of important documents. These documents, which figured prominently in the Peruvian government's decision to break with Cuba at the end of December, represent the clearest proof to date of the intent and extent of Fidel Castro's activities in Latin America.

Despite their importance, they have received surprisingly little publicity in the United States. Among the papers obtained there was a confidential letter written to the Cuban Foreign Ministry by Luis Ricardo Alonso, Castro's ambas-

sador to Peru. It is, in Alonso's words, a "Report of Political
Expenses," including an accounting of "international funds"
given to the Peruvian Communist party, "which in its turn
has supplied me with reports concerning the work it is carrying on throughout Peru in defense of the Cuban revolution." In the process of listing his expenditures ($15,000 a
month for the embassy's own propaganda and subversive
activities, another $15,000 worth of "international funds" for
the Reds), Alonso makes the following comments:

In accordance with instructions received from the Minister of
the Armed Forces, Commandante Raúl Castro, I have been oc-
cupying myself directly with the organization of insurrectional
groups in conjunction with the Communist Party and Apra Rebelde [a rabidly pro-Castro splinter group of the large, noncommunist APRA party], as well as with other friends of the Left,
all of whom are ready for anything in case the announced imperialist invasion of Cuba takes place. . . .
    I am absolutely convinced that the work we are carrying out
. . . is the most positive possible, notwithstanding the scrutiny to
which I am being constantly subjected by the Military Intelligence Service. Thanks to very valuable contacts and reports. . . I
have been able to develop the entire plan drawn up in Havana
. . . Peru must be considered as a center of the defense against
capitalism, given its geographic location; the economic, political,
and social conflicts which we can intensify; and the tension created by the agitation which exists between Peru and Ecuador
because of the border problem. . . .
    They tell me in the Department of Latin-American Affairs of
our Foreign Ministry that the technical advisers of the Soviet
Union and Popular China [sic] have great hopes for the work
going on in Peru. . . . This is because we are not only attacking
an oligarchic government that is in the service of yanqui imperialism, but also because we are unmasking APRA and assuming
the revolutionary leadership of the students, workers, and peasants, in order to bind them resolutely to the Cuban Revolution.

Some of Alonso's observations taken from earlier memos and reports are equally enlightening. A sampling of these:

I am maintaining correspondence—not through the mails—with our ambassador in Quito, Mariano Rodríguez, as well as with the Ecuadorian ambassador in Lima. Through the good offices of both, we are continuing to strengthen contacts between the Ecuadorian and Peruvian students who attended the conference commemorating our most patriotic and revolutionary date [26th of July].

I am following instructions with regard to the Treaty of Rio [the 1942 border treaty between Ecuador and Peru which Ecuadorian President José María Velasco Ibarra now considers invalid] though I do not think it practical or convenient to make known here in Peru that our position is in favor of Ecuador, because we would then lose all that we have gained.

I have the honor to comply with your request [the man making the request in this case being Raúl Castro] for information concerning the Peruvian Army ... given me by Dr. Armando Hart, Minister of Education of the Revolutionary Government, who came to this capital to attend the Seventh American Congress of Educators.... The Peruvian Army is a very disciplined force, with an officer corps similar to that of Batista, except for the fact that these are career men. There is great esprit de corps ... great respect for the officers among the troops.

However [military], conspiracies do occur almost continually. ... They involve followers of Odria [ex-President Manuel Odria] or those linked with such other groups as Popular Action.... These and other officers, though they act in different interests, can serve our ends in the matter of political infiltration.

Other evidence of international subversive activity on the part of the Castro government was later uncovered in Argentina, which resulted in the closure of Castro's so-called "news agency," Prensa Latina.

This international wire service, staffed by known Communists in many places, is subsidized by the Cuban government. When the Buenos Aires police raided Prensa Latina's office they found files which seemed to connect the agency with an aborted revolt of Argentine extremists. The Peruvian government also found Prensa Latina disseminating subversive propaganda and shut its Lima office.

In October, 1960, the Inter-American Press Association denounced Prensa Latina and in November the Inter-American Association of Broadcasters said Castro's Prensa Latina was "a vehicle in the service of international communism."

After the Seventh Meeting of Consultation of Ministers of Foreign Affairs at San José, Costa Rica, where United States Secretary of State Christian Herter was unable to persuade the Latin ministers even to mention Cuba by name in the Declaration of San José, which denounced the "intervention or threat of intervention of an extracontinental power in the affairs of the American republics," Castro practically dissociated himself from the inter-American system and followed a bellicose path toward the other American republics.

Fidel could have pretended to ignore the San José Declaration as it did not specifically mention Cuba, but he chose to strike back at both the United States and the Organization of American States. For days radio, television, newspaper advertisements, and posters all over Cuba invited the people to take part in a "People's Assembly" in Havana. This assembly took place in the Civic Plaza where Castro loves to have people congregate in order to practice his much-publicized "direct democracy." More than half a million habaneros and guajiros, brought by truck and train from all over the island, attended the General Assembly of the People of Cuba, as this meeting was officially named.

After denouncing Yankee imperialism and calling the Organization of American States the "Ministry of Colonies" of the United States government, Castro asked the crowd—which had kept up a continual chant of "Cuba yes, Yankee no"—if it would approve the establishment of diplomatic relations with the People's Republic of China, a country which, he said, no nation in Latin America has dared to recognize. The mob answered, "Sí, sí, sí." Replied Castro, "We hereby break relations with the puppet regime of Chiang Kai-shek."

After declaring that Cuba would never attack the United States naval base at Guantánamo for the reason that it would give the United States a pretext to invade Cuba, Castro held aloft a copy of the 1952 Cuba-United States Mutual Defense Treaty and tore it up before the eyes of the crowd. He then did the same thing to the two-week-old Declaration of San José. After tearing it up Castro began reading a rather long document condemning both the United States and the OAS. He stated that this document would be known as the "Declaration of Havana" and that it was the reply of the Cuban people to the Declaration of San José.

Shortly after proclaiming the Declaration of Havana on September 2, 1960, which millions of Cubans signed, Fidel left for the United States to attend the United Nations General Assembly, where he did all he could to impress upon world opinion the fact that Cuba had become a new member of the Soviet bloc. He met every head of state of the communist and neutralist countries and was warmly greeted and embraced by Prime Minister Nikita Khrushchev.

In a four-hour and 26-minute speech, the longest ever delivered before the United Nations General Assembly, Castro charged that the United States "monopolies turned Cuba into a colony," and took the Soviet position on every issue, from the Soviet proposal to recognize Patrice Lumumba as the only leader of the Congo to the admission of Red China into the United Nations. "We support seating the true representative of the Chinese people" declared Castro, after assailing the government of Chiang Kai-shek. He bitterly attacked both presidential candidates, Kennedy and Nixon, to the extent that the General Assembly President, Patrick Boland, had to ask him to stop.

Upon his return to Cuba Castro right off embarked on the intensification of his hate campaign against the United States. He also made an all-out effort to "free" other Latin-American countries from Yankee "imperialism."

During November three Central American countries— Guatemala, Nicaragua, and Costa Rica—were the scenes of disturbances and in each case there were charges of Cuban complicity. In Guatemala army units revolted against President Miguel Ydigoras Fuentes and seized Puerto Barrios, 150 miles northeast of the capital on the Atlantic coast. President Ydigoras ordered a state of siege throughout the country and was able to squelch the revolt. The planes used by President Ydigoras to put down that rebellion at Puerto Barrios belonged to the anti-Castro Cuban Liberation Air Force and were piloted by Cubans.

In Nicaragua there was also a sort of revolt and for two days rebels held two small towns just south of Managua, the capital. And in Costa Rica the government prevented an attack against Nicaragua by a group of rebels.

Both the Guatemalan and Nicaraguan governments claim they have proof that Cuba was directly involved in these rebel activities. At the time it was reported that both governments were planning to ask the Organization of American States to invoke the Rio de Janeiro Treaty of 1947 (Inter-American Treaty of Reciprocal Assistance). This treaty stipulates that an attack on one of the American republics shall be regarded as "an attack on all." It also provides for sanctions against the aggressor. However, the Eisenhower administration realized that the majority of the Latin-American countries were at the time still not in favor of taking any action against Fidel Castro, and consequently the governments of Guatemala and Nicaragua never brought the matter before the OAS.

Nevertheless, the United States took steps to block any Cuban efforts to spread its revolution. Eisenhower ordered United States naval units to patrol the Caribbean coasts of Guatemala and Nicaragua in order to prevent the landing of armed forces or supplies from abroad.

Despite the announcement by a State Department official that the United States naval forces would render assistance to Guatemala and Nicaragua only if those countries requested it, the reaction in Latin America to the United States move was unfavorable. For example, *El Tiempo,* Colombia's largest newspaper, and generally pro-United States, said "it disturbs us profoundly" that the action was taken without taking into account the Organization of American States. Mexico's *Ultimas Noticias* said the "action was inopportune and would probably provoke anti-Americanism."

All the Western Hemisphere leftist newspapers followed the government-controlled press and radio of Cuba, bitterly attacking the United States action. Some of these newspapers repeated the lines of *Revolución* that President Eisenhower's utilization of the United States naval power off the coast of Central America was "the first step in a plan to invade Cuba and a flagrant example of Yankee military intervention in the Caribbean."

The Soviet Union attacked the United States in similar

terms. Moscow radio said the United States action was "fraught with the danger of a military conflict" and the communist Chinese Premier Chou En-lai chimed in with a denunciation of the "brazen" United States decision "to threaten Cuba further by force of arms."

The State Department, on its part, issued a statement charging that the communist bloc of nations had contributed to tension in the Caribbean "by burdening the Cuban economy with excessive arms purchases and by supporting the aggressive policies" of the Castro regime. The State Department said further that Cuba had received at least 28,000 tons of arms from the Soviet bloc. It said Castro has built an armed military force "larger than any army in Latin America" and ten times bigger than the force of former President Batista.

However, Castro's No. 1 target was not Central America but oil-rich Venezuela, where the United States has five times the investment it had in Cuba, and which is strategically located for blocking the Panama Canal.

In Venezuela the United States has at stake the iron ore that feeds mills of the United States Steel Fairless plant opposite Trenton, New Jersey, and Bethlehem's Sparrows Point plant near Baltimore, and which arrives daily from the great Orinoco mines. The United States has billions invested in wells, rigs, and refineries in the Maracaibo region, one of the greatest oil fields in the world.

A Fidelista regime in Caracas would mean a terrific defeat for the United States, as Venezuela is important not only for its resources but for its strategic position commanding the approach both to the Caribbean sea lanes and south to Brazil.

After a year of relations strained to the breaking point

because of the open support given by Cuba to Venezuelan extremists and insurrectionist groups, President Rómulo Betancourt announced on November 10, 1961, that there was no other possible reply to the insults of the Castro regime than a diplomatic break.

Venezuela's diplomatic break with Cuba was significant because it was the first of the liberal governments, which once gave tacit or open support to the Cuban revolution, to break with the Castro regime. It was significant, too, because it followed by only a few hours the request by Colombia to the Organization of American States for a new conference of foreign ministers to deal with Castro's Cuba on the basis of threats posed "by the intervention of extracontinental powers," meaning, of course, Cuba's military ties with the Soviet Union, Red China, and other nations of the Communist bloc.

In announcing Venezuela's break, President Betancourt denounced as a risk to hemispheric peace any country that molds its foreign policy on that of extracontinental powers, and pointed out that the 300,000 strong, heavily armed Castro militia is the largest military force in the Western Hemisphere outside the United States.

Fidel Castro's subversive attempts to overthrow the constitutional government of President Rómulo Betancourt began shortly after the Meeting of Consultation of Ministers of Foreign Affairs at San José, Costa Rica. Venezuelan Foreign Minister Ignacio Luis Arcaya, refused to sign the watered-down resolution against communist penetration in Latin America which did not even mention Cuba by name. Betancourt was forced to order his foreign minister home from the meeting, and gave instructions to the second-in-command to sign the resolution for Venezuela. Upon his return to Caracas,

Arcaya was relieved of his post and Castro agents intensified their activities with the leftists. Extreme leftists and radicals suddenly became affluent. They spent more money than they had ever had before and it was obvious they were preparing for a coup. At the end of October demonstrations flared up in Caracas, in Coro, a seaport in western Venezuela where the army took control, and in Ciudad Bolívar in the eastern part of the country on the Orinoco River.

A Cabinet reorganization was requested by the Republic Democratic Union (URD), second largest party in Betancourt's coalition government. The URD has a strong following in Caracas and is no doubt infiltrated by both Castro and communist agents. One of them, thirty-two-year-old ex-journalist Fabricio Ojeda, is a congressman and a ranking member of the Military Affairs Committee of the Venezuelan Chamber of Deputies.

I met Ojeda in Cuba, where he goes every other month to see Fidel, Raúl Castro, Major Guevara, and other bigwigs. I am quite certain that he is a Marxist and a revolutionary dedicated to the cause of Fidelismo, and he has been made an honorary officer in Fidel's army. As a member of the Military Affairs Committee he spends a great part of his time selling Fidelismo to young Venezuelan army officers. If the constitutional government of President Betancourt has been able to squelch every attempt of the left to gain power by force, it has been due to a great extent to the opposition of the army officers to leftist radicalism and communism.

On the other hand, there is always the possibility of a military coup d'état. Since the downfall of the Pérez Jiménez dictatorship in 1958 there have been many abortive military coups, all of which, so far, have failed because of the loyalty of the majority of the army officers and a swift mobilization of labor, which immediately declared a general strike in protest against the threat of a military coup. In every instance of the calling of a general strike by the Confederation of Venezuelan Workers (Confederación de Trabajadores de Venezuela) which is dominated by President Betancourt's party, Acción Democrática, it has had the support of the employers.

It has been reported that Ojeda was the brain behind the leftist riots of October, November, and December. The rioting leftists were accused by President Betancourt of trying to touch off a Castro-style revolution in Venezuela. Betancourt won the test, but revolution is still in the air and it is very difficult to foretell what will become of this country where armed students several times barricaded themselves in the university, chanting Castro slogans, and where leftist newspapers and publications are constantly urging a Cuban-style revolt. Yet it was significant that during the November and December disturbances the leftist rebels who called Caracas University "Little Stalingrad" were unable to gain popular support. Hopeful calls for a general strike went unheeded and when the government finally besieged the University with troops the radical students surrendered.

Cuba's complicity was in the open. Shortly after President Betancourt dismissed his foreign minister for refusing to sign the Declaration of San José the DIGEPOL (Venezuela's secret police) raided the headquarters of the 26th of July Movement in Caracas. They found evidence, as they had in Lima, that the Cuban government through its embassy in Caracas was financing subversive activities and that two of the more radical newspapers—*Tribuna Popular,* the official communist newspaper, and the weekly *Izquierda* (Left), the official publication of the Revolutionary Left Movement con-

sidered by many to be the offspring of the Communist party
—were receiving financial aid from the Cuban Embassy.

It is significant that several weeks before the November
riots there appeared in *Izquierda* an article by Congressman
Domingo Alberto Rangel, openly advocating a general strike
and a people's uprising against the Betancourt government.
After the publication of this article *Izquierda* was closed
by the government, which also expelled from the country
Francisco Rene Chacón, representative in Caracas of *Revolución,* the official Castro newspaper in Cuba. According to
DIGEPOL, Chacón was involved in the attempted seizure
of Radio Rumbos, in order to put on the air a tape-recorded
announcement that the Betancourt administration had been
succeeded by a people's government. Fabricio Ojeda also
took part in this incident.

The Cuban charge d'affaires in Caracas, Guillermo León
Antich, with whom I worked closely in the Foreign Office in
Havana, was declared persona non grata by the Venezuelan
government. From the time of our association in the Foreign
Office León Antich was known as Raúl Castro's trusted man,
and it was rumored that he had been planted in the Foreign
Office to spy on Foreign Minister Roberto Agramonte. As a
matter of fact Dr. Agramonte relieved him of his duties as
private secretary because he had delivered, without Agramonte's consent, the secret files of the Foreign Minister's
private office to the G-2, Castro's military intelligence.

Although President Betancourt appears to have strong support from the labor unions, the army, the police, and the
majority of the people, Venezuela's troubles continue to
brew. This oil-rich South American nation is too big for Castro and the Communists to let go. Castro's appeal is still
running high in Venezuela, especially in Caracas where are

concentrated all the radicals who demand alliance with Cuba, nationalization of foreign oil companies, and radical land reform on the Cuban pattern, instead of the careful system of land distribution and organized rural credit being carried out by the Betancourt administration through legislative action by the Congress.

A Castro take-over in Venezuela would have a profound impact on United States diplomatic and economic standing in Latin America. Officials in the State Department and in the American Embassy in Caracas make no attempt to minimize their apprehension that a Castro-type regime in Venezuela would embolden leftist forces in the rest of Latin America.

Diplomats all over Latin America believe that a new test of strength between the popularly elected government of President Betancourt, which is friendly to the United States, and the leftist group will occur in the near future. In the beginning of the summer of 1961 it was announced that the Venezuelan government had intercepted several tons of arms —Czech submachine guns, ammunition, grenades—shipped from Cuba to isolated points along the Venezuelan coast.

This smuggling of arms coincided with the Castroite attempts to overthrow the leftist reform government of President Paz Estenssoro of Bolivia. It was reported by the Bolivian authorities that the plot, which was supposed to begin with a "hunger march" on the capital by striking leftist tin miners, was hatched in the Cuban Embassy at La Paz together with local Communists. La Paz has been, after Caracas, one of the main centers of Fidelism. There is a strong Fidelista current within the national revolutionary movement of President Paz Estenssoro, which has been carrying out a social reform but less extensive or complete than

in Cuba. The Bolivian revolution has been socialist orientated and United States financial and technical aid has kept
it from collapsing. Anti-American sentiment has been created
by the Cuban ambassador, who financed anti-Yankee demonstrations on the July 26th anniversary of Castro's revolutionary movement. Picturesque evidence of Castro's inroads in
Bolivia is Feldman Velarde, Bolivia's Minister of Education
who is also La Paz correspondent of Castro's Prensa Latina
news agency.

There is not a single week that some Castroite activity is
not reported in Latin America. During riots in Venezuela
against President Betancourt and the uprisings in Central
America, the governments of Argentina, Chile, and Brazil
were also contending against general strikes, which officials
said were encouraged by Castro agents. Violence also flared
in Panama, Ecuador, Colombia, and even in Mexico, where
former President Cárdenas has been talking of the need of
a second revolution in his country and strongly supporting
all Castro initiatives. He was the chief sponsor of the so-
called Latin-American Conference for National Sovereignty,
Economic Emancipation and Peace, which was held in
March, 1961, in Mexico City. This conference condemned:

The OAS as "an instrument of North American imperialist
penetration among the peoples of Latin America which never has
fulfilled nor can fulfill what it set out to do."

Multilateral or bilateral treaties and agreements which revive
the Monroe Doctrine, including the San José, Costa Rica, declaration condemning "extracontinental intervention" and the Rio de
Janeiro agreement that an attack on any American state is an
attack on all.

Military pacts and missions, economic and technical missions,
and press groups such as the Inter-American Press Association
(which was meeting simultaneously in Acapulco).

The "ideology of anticommunism as an attempt to divide peoples and for imperialist penetration."

Cárdenas has also been the main obstacle to any policy that might hurt Castro. Although President López Mateos' administration has put down pro-Castro student riots and it has been reported that he is cool to Fidel Castro himself, Mexico's Foreign Ministry is under control of a splinter group which adheres to former President Cárdenas' attitude toward Castro.

Most of these splinter leaders are stationed outside of Mexico on diplomatic assignments. Mexico's OAS delegation is pro-Cárdenas, and none other than the ambassador himself, Vicente Sánchez Gavito, in a recent OAS meeting labeled Castro's Cuba as the "green canefield of New World hope." Mexico's position in the OAS has been a major factor in the failure of all United States efforts to bring about at least a censure resolution against Castro.

Furthermore, Castro seems most interested in making out of Mexico his first bulwark against anticommunism. One of his best diplomats, José Antonio Portuondo, is the Cuban ambassador to Mexico, and he is pushing Cuba's propaganda with great intensity. Some twenty-six diplomatic pouches reach Mexico from Cuba every day. The Soviet Embassy ships in thirty pouches loaded with Cuban propaganda, and Ambassador Portuondo is a frequent visitor to Soviet Ambassador Vladimir I. Bazikin.

The Mexican government is fully aware of the Cuban-Soviet diplomatic activities. Since there is nothing illegal about them, the López Mateos administration merely maintains surveillance. There are indications, however, that Mexico is edging away from Castro. A growing number of Mexicans are becoming aware that pro-Castro demonstrations are drying up the inflow of both U.S. private capital and American tourism. On September 1, 1961, President López Mateos announced, in his State of the Union message delivered before Congress, that the cornerstone of Mexican foreign policy now rests on close relations with the United States. Diplomatic observers in Mexico City interpreted López Mateos' message as a basic shift away from Castro and toward Washington.

In Brazil, the key country in the United States $20 billion Alliance for Progress program for rebuilding Latin America, the leftward drift was frightening during the seven months in office of eccentric Jânio Quadros, who inexplicably resigned the presidency on August 25, 1961, and pushed his country to the brink of civil war.

Brazil, the fourth largest country in the world, with half of South America's 140 million population, was traditionally Washington's best friend in Latin America. She was the only Latin country in this hemisphere that sent an expeditionary force to fight the Axis powers in World War II. But under Quadros this close cooperation with Washington suddenly changed. From the time of his inauguration on January 30, 1961, Senhor Quadros left no stone unturned to show his political independence of the United States and his affinity to the so-called "uncommitted" nations. When President Kennedy offered an immediate $100 million loan to help him through his first ninety days in office, he turned it down and sent economic missions behind the Iron Curtain in search of trade. He established diplomatic relations with Rumania, Bulgaria, Hungary, and even with Albania. He was about to resume diplomatic relations with the Soviet Union. A $56 million trade-credit agreement with Red China was concluded in Peiping by controversial Vice-President João Goulart before leaving for Brazil to assume the presidency.

It should be underscored, however, that shortly after his icy rejection of President Kennedy's emergency loan Quadros accepted not only the $100 million stop-gap credit but a billion dollars' worth of United States aid. When he resigned, the United States had already programmed almost $2 billion in aid and credit under the Alliance for Progress program. Yet in his letter of resignation Quadros said that he was unable to carry on because of the pressure of "ambitious groups and individuals, domestic and foreign," which was inevitably interpreted as an indictment of Washington.

As far as the Cuban issue was concerned, Quadros was a monkey wrench in the OAS machinery in any action against the Castro regime. When Adolf A. Berle, Jr., then chief of President Kennedy's Latin-American task force, went to Brasilia seeking Brazil's cooperation, or at least forbearance in United States attempts to depose Castro, Quadros said that intervention was repugnant to him in any nation and in any form. Later, when Minister of Finance Clemente Mariani was in Washington negotiating United States financial aid, Quadros issued a note violently condemning any kind of intervention—military, economic, or political. Even during the Alliance for Progress economic meeting in Punta del Este, Uruguay, Quadros instructed Senhor Mariani to commend formally the "constructive work of the Cuban Delegation." After the meeting Che Guevara, Cuba's chief delegate, went to Brasilia, where Quadros awarded him the Grand Cross of the Order of Cruceiro do Sol, the highest decoration bestowed by that country. Significantly, the same day that Quadros was presenting Guevara with Brazil's highest decoration the governor of the important state of Guanabara,

Carlos Lacerda, was presenting the key to the city of Rio de Janeiro to Dr. Manuel Antonio de Varona, one of the leading foes of the Castro regime.

Upon Quadros' resignation, military leaders openly challenged the right of Brazil's left-wing vice-president, João Goulart, to accede to the presidency, and the country was threatened with civil war. Goulart, a wealthy landowner from southern Brazil, is a very controversial figure in Brazil's political spectrum and his communist sympathies are plainly on the record. His leftist leanings were the cause of the military opposition to his becoming president of the country. However, the crisis was solved without the loss of a single life, without one shot being fired. A compromise between the military and the Goulart forces was worked out through a constitutional amendment limiting the executive power of the president. This compromise was made to appease the military, which threatened to bar Goulart from the presidency—if necessary, by force.

After backstage maneuvering, Brazil became a European-style parliamentary democracy. Goulart became president, with most of his powers curtailed, and a mild conservative, Tancredo Neves, was appointed prime minister and formed a middle-of-the-road coalition government. The aim of the sponsors of the change was to give the real power to the Prime Minister, with Senhor Goulart succeeding to the presidency as a figurehead.

Where Brazil goes from here is difficult to foresee. Senhor Neves, who is supposed to be the real power in the new constitutional setup, said, "We are going to start anew," and predicted a foreign policy of "pure tradition"—taken to mean that he will reverse the Quadros trend toward closer links with Cuba and the Soviet bloc. Pending are proposed trade deals with Iron Curtain countries, the question of renewing diplomatic relations with the Soviet Union, and a trade pact with Fidel Castro.

As important as the problem of foreign relations is Brazil's precarious economic situation. Quadros' efforts to reform Brazil's economy had Washington support. This may seem ironic in view of Washington's concern over Quadros' flirtation with Cuba, but United States policy makers were so convinced that Quadros alone could bring some order to Brazil's chronically chaotic economy that his friendship toward the Reds and his pointed insistence on a strictly "independent" foreign policy were largely ignored. And the United States was counting on a strong Brazil as a leader in the Alliance for Progress.

It should be noted, however, that Quadros' endeavors to enact a fair proportionate income tax law, to reform the currency and overhaul the bureaucracy, and even his land reform were facing a snowballing opposition in the Congress, which is now the most important political body in Brazil's new system of government.

It is highly significant that some of the critics of Quadros' policy are already repenting. This is the case of Carlos Lacerda, a Communist in his youth and now a diehard anti-Communist, who was one of Quadros' earliest supporters and recently the most prominent opposer of his pro-Cuba and neutralist policy. When Quadros resigned, Lacerda's comment was that it was "lamentable and not desired by anyone."

One of the most remarkable of the results of Quadros' surprising resignation has been the emergence in Brazil of the ruling elite which held a monopoly of political power from the days of the late Getulio Vargas until the Quadros land-

slide last year. Goulart rose to power as a self-styled political
heir of the former Brazilian strong man; the present prime
minister, Dr. Tancredo Neves, was minister of justice under
Vargas. And one of the strongest parties in Brazil's Congress,
the Social Democrats, is that of former President Juscelino
Kubitschek. Both the Social Democrats and Goulart's Labor
party were founded during the regime of Vargas, who dominated Brazil's political life for two decades, until his death
by suicide in 1954.

The Vargas clique was characterized not by honesty but
by graft. A crisis with the military created over the scandals
in government and the rising corruption while the pro-Var-
gas forces were in power are now a matter of anxiety among
the more enlightened political and military leaders. They are
concerned about the willingness and ability of the new parliamentary government of former Vargas "widows," as they
are called in Brazil, to carry out social reforms and lead the
country on a sound economic development program as suggested by President Kennedy's Alliance for Progress.

While it is true that democratic and constitutional institutions have been saved by the compromise between the
Goulart followers and the military, it is also true that Brazil's
revolutionary potentialities still remain. The carrying out of
economic and social reforms is imperative to prevent a
major revolutionary upsurge which might plunge the country into chaos and eventually into communist domination.
Although not officially recognized, the Communist party in
Brazil is strong and there is no doubt that Castroism poses
a potential threat to the country, particularly to its north-
eastern part—a tremendous area of impoverishment that has
starved while the country's ruling class waxed fat. This vast,
remote, and poverty-ridden corner of Brazil is dangerously

threatened by an emerging peasant revolt led by Francisco Julião, a forty-three-year-old socialist deputy in the Pernambuco state legislature at Recife, who preaches drastic land reforms and proclaims the virtues of Fidel Castro and Mao Tse-tung. Julião is the author of a booklet in which he promises that "the cruel latifundium" will perish in Brazil as it did in Castro's Cuba and Communist China. He was in Havana and in Peiping in the fall of 1960, and his visit to China coincided with that of Che Guevara.

It is very significant that on August 29, 1961, at the height of the Brazilian crisis, Fidel Castro urged the masses to take the matter into their own hands to prevent "reactionary militarists" from installing an "illegal fascist regime." In a televised speech, Castro said:

If the Brazilian people make use of Cuba's experience and take arms and throw themselves into the fight in the mountains, jungles and forests, the reactionaries will never be able to succeed.

If workers, peasants, students and progressive people and honest military men take up arms and organize not one front but a thousand fronts, never will the military reactionaries be able to defeat them.

It is a fact that the United States and the noncommunist world has an important stake in Brazil. A major upheaval could have been formidable and perhaps catastrophic to the rest of Latin America. Washington and the democratic leadership in many of the Latin-American countries are jointly and individually engaged in what may well be the last effort to convince the underprivileged masses that the hemisphere's future lies in the democratic system, bolstered by an effective attack on poverty and underdevelopment, which are the main goals of President Kennedy's Alliance for Progress, and not in the Castro brand of revolutionary "socialism."

In Chile also Castroism is as strong as in Brazil and Venezuela. When Castro sent relief to victims of the 1960 earth-
quakes in Chile, astonished Chilean officials found that bags
of sugar and piles of clothing were intermixed with propaganda leaflets and booklets, one of which was Major Guevara's *Guerrilla Warfare*, containing a blueprint for revolution.

None other than Senator Salvador Allende, runner-up to
President Alessandri Rodríguez in the 1958 presidential race,
is the chief sponsor of Fidelismo in Chile. Like many other
left-wing politicians, Allende is a frequent visitor to Cuba
and a close associate of Raúl Castro. On one of his many
visits to Havana I met him and he impressed me as being a
dedicated Marxist who would have no hesitation in communizing Chile if he ever got to power. Allende is the sponsor
of a bill to nationalize the country's copper-mining industry,
which is nearly 90 per cent American owned.

Colombia is a tinderbox. The unceasing guerrilla warfare
that rages through the mountain passes in certain areas of
this strategic country on the southern flank of the Panama
Canal, a remnant of years of civil war between Liberals and
Conservatives, has been speeded-up by communists and
agents of Fidel Castro.

The Conservative party newspaper *El Siglo*, owned by
Laureano Gómez, former president of the Republic, recently
published a map of eleven "independent republics" which it
reports that the guerrillas have set up across the country.
Most of these "republics" are under control of communists
and sympathizers of Castro's Cuba.

The nation's leading newspaper and voice of the Liberal
party, *El Tiempo*, urged President Alberto Lleras to take immediate action against the guerrillas. The Lleras administra-

tion has been conducting a police action against the roaming guerrilla forces, but it is a long way from wiping them out altogether. Lack of adequate roads and the division of the country by towering mountain ranges have made it difficult for government troops to penetrate the guerrilla infested areas, which according to the *El Siglo* map are extended from the plains across the Andes ranges to the Gulf of Uraba near the Panama border.

At the request of the Colombian government, the United States has been supplying Colombia's armed forces with modern small arms, ammunition, and equipment, including helicopters, for operations against the guerrillas.

Ecuador is another striking example of the strong influence Castroism still has. The riots and demonstrations that preceded the fall of President Velasco Ibarra in November, 1961, were the work to some extent of communist agitators and Cuban agents. The head of Cuba's diplomatic mission in Quito had been expelled by the outgoing President. Significantly, the new President, Carlos Julio Arosemena, an aristocrat turned leftist who flew to Moscow at the time Stevenson was visiting Ecuador, said that as far as he knew Ecuador had not broken relations with Cuba and "if it has they will be renewed."

The ouster of José María Velasco Ibarra as President of Ecuador is a lesson for Latin-American demagogues. Velasco Ibarra, a crusty caudillo of the old Latin-American school, sailed into office on the wings of half-baked leftist promises. He kept the pot boiling by resurrecting an old border dispute with Peru and flirting with Moscow and Havana.

Velasco Ibarra's slow and corrupt administration wasn't able to fulfill campaign promises and unrest built up. Some of his original backers, like Vice-President Arosemena, took up Fidelismo as the answer to the nation's social problems. Velasco Ibarra turned right and charged that his second-in-command, leftist Arosemena, had been plotting a "Communist take-over." But many officers of the armed forces felt that the old man was too inept to fend off the threat from the left and deposed him, promptly installing the Chief Justice of the Supreme Court.

Ecuador's Congress and Air Force then entered the picture on behalf of Vice-President Arosemena. Congress in a special session named him chief executive. Air force jets flew over Quito, discharged their machine guns and a few light bombs, and Arosemena, the new demagogue, took over.

In Washington, as usual, the State Department adopted a "wait-and-see" attitude. But in Havana, the tune was different. "This is another victory over Yankee imperialism. It must have hit Washington like a 65-megaton bomb," said Castro.

In the Dominican Republic, where finally all the Trujillo clan left the island, there is always the threat that the Communists from Cuba will move in, taking control not only of the Dominican Republic but also of Haiti.

It was very significant that the Castro government assailed the United States in both the Security Council of the United Nations and the Council of the Organization of American States for sending warships and aircraft to the coastal waters of the Dominican Republic during the frustrated attempt of the brothers of the late dictator Rafael L. Trujillo, Héctor and Arismendi, to restore the iron-clad dictatorship.

According to the Cuban complaints, the United States planned to land the Marines in the Dominican Republic to uphold the last vestiges of the dictatorship and prevent a real people's revolution.

On the other hand, Cuba's agents inside the Dominican Republic have been urging the overthrow of President Balaguer, who is dismissed as a puppet of Yankee imperialism, totally lacking in popular support, alien to the nation's interests, and backed only by the bayonets of the reactionary ruling class.

The threat of Castroism has even reached European possessions in the Western Hemisphere. British Guiana, the strategic colony bordering Venezuela and Brazil, might become another Cuba and the first beachhead on the mainland of South America. Dr. Chedde B. Jagan and his extreme leftist People's Progressive party won their expected victory in the August 21, 1961, elections. Dr. Jagan and his Chicago-born wife, Janet Rosenberg Jagan, have been labeled by top American and British officials as communist in everything but name.

Back in 1953 the Jagans also led their People's Progressive party to a victory at the polls. But the British government six months later ousted Jagan and his five leftist associates by an official order that said they were "prepared to go to any length, including violence, to turn British Guiana into a communist state." The Jagans won another election in 1957 but the British kept control of the colony. At that time Jagan became minister of transportation.

Dr. Jagan's victory in August, 1961, is especially significant because the British government has committed itself to granting full independence to this colony of diamonds, bauxite, sugar, and widespread poverty in one year from the date of the election. It is certain that Jagan's first move as prime minister of British Guiana will be to request full independence for his country.

Jagan and his fiery wife might indeed cause serious trouble

to the United States and to the other Latin-American countries. Not only are the Jagans far to the left politically, but they have also had a close relationship with Fidel Castro. On several occasions Jagan has gone to Cuba to visit Castro, and he has received loans from the Castro government which have amounted to more than $8 million; on the eve of the 1961 elections Castro agreed to buy 7 million board feet of Guiana timber and 250,000 railroad ties.

It is difficult to foresee what policy Jagan will ultimately follow although he has rejected charges that his victory would mean communist domination of Guiana. In letters quoted in the *New York Times* during the campaign Jagan pledged himself to adhere to the principles of parliamentary democracy. He also expressed his desire and expectation to link Guiana economically to the hemispheric system, and it has been reported that one of Jagan's ambitions is to have his country benefit from President Kennedy's Alliance for Progress.

Jagan visited Washington in October, 1961, and had a 90-minute meeting with President Kennedy—half an hour longer than scheduled—at the White House. Speaking before the National Press Club, Jagan disclosed that he had described to the President his program for a 240-million-dollar-development plan, to be financed largely by outside aid. Jagan also said that he would like to get a substantial part of this sum from the United States, but that he would accept aid from the Soviet bloc if it is not forthcoming from the West.

Fresh back in British Guiana from his trip to Washington, Jagan first announced that the United States refused him financial help, and then, a few days later, that United States and Canadian aid were on the way "in spite of our trade relationship with Cuba."

In Washington there is little eagerness to help an outspoken Marxist seeking aid with threats. But the fear is that refusal might force him deeper into the Soviet orbit. A familiar problem of the cold-war in the hemisphere.

In spite of all this there is still great concern in London and Washington as to the course Jagan will actually take. The real concern is strategic. Owing to his country's proximity to Venezuela and Brazil, British Guiana holds an ideal geographic position toward becoming a staging area for Castro's communist operations in both those countries.

Summarizing, signs of Castro's inroads appear in every country of Latin America. The fact is that to many of Latin America's poor, many of the region's frustrated people, many of its intellectually and ideologically confused, and to the masses that have never been able to enjoy the benefits of a democratic society, communism and Fidelism are a bright and attractive hope. The unfortunate fact is not that the Communists, some of the left-wingers, and many of the uneducated and landless peasants give Castro their unswerving support, but that most of the politicians who would like to see Castro removed from the scene hesitate to sympathize openly with the United States efforts to topple the communist government of Cuba through a collective action of the Organization of American States.

For the United States the prospects in Latin America are not overly bright and the situation is not one in which Washington can, doing this or that, produce an overnight change by its own effort. The growing strength of Castroism in Latin America and the possibility of the emergence of a communist state in British Guiana are problems of vital concern to the

free world today. Even more disturbing is the neutralist policy of Brazil, and the continuing opposition from some of the
key Latin-American governments to join the United States
in strong, concerted action against the Castro regime—though
everyone recognizes the danger of a communist Cuba.

CHAPTER VII

The Anti-Castro Forces

EVERY true revolution breeds its counterrevolutionaries. The Castro revolution is no exception, although most of the anti-Castro Cubans object to the word "counterrevolutionary" as they turned against him only when his revolution turned communist.

[When Castro moved into Havana in January, 1959, he had practically the entire Cuban population solidly behind him. He was a national hero, and even some Batistianos wanted to get aboard his bandwagon. But soon many people, including some who had fought in the hills with him against Batista, became suspicious of his ultimate aims. As early as the spring of 1959 many Cuban leaders began to suspect that the Castro reforms were following a communist pattern and they were shocked by the rumors of communist infiltration in the rebel army.] These fears were to a great extent confirmed when Major Hubert Matos resigned his commission in that army, expressing similar concern.

Yet Fidel Castro had the support of the overwhelming majority of the Cuban people during the first year of his administration. In the early months the only people opposing his government were Batista's henchmen and some of the extremely wealthy, who were apprehensive of the revolution in itself. Most of them were big landowners affected by the agrarian reform, whom the Cubans called siquitril-lados (cicatrized one—literally, a fighting cock that has been mortally wounded in a fight by the breaking of its breast-bone).

Most of Castro's opponents were exiled to the neighboring countries of Cuba, including the United States. The majority of them were of the Batista clique who had enriched themselves by outright corruption, by selling concessions, and in countless other ways. Also some army officers and police accused of atrocities had been able to get out of the country.

One of the first Batistianos to organize an anti-Castro group in the United States was Rafael Díaz Balart, the leader of the "White Rose" group, an extremist pro-Batista faction that was organized as early as January, 1959, in New York City.

The White Rose went so far as to choose a provisional president of Cuba for the day that Castro was overthrown. Another Batista henchman very active at that time was the former Cuban ambassador to the United Nations, Emilio Núñez Portuondo. He established his headquarters in Washington and began putting out a weekly publication, *Latin American Events*, in the form of a newsletter dedicated to painting the Cuban revolution as a communist undertaking.

Ambassador Núñez Portuondo had many connections with high officials of the Eisenhower administration in Washington. He tried, unsuccessfully, through his old friend and colleague, Henry Cabot Lodge, former United States ambassador to the United Nations, to get the support of the White House for an invasion of Cuba by former officers and men of Batista's army. To head such an invasion Núñez Portuondo chose General Pedraza.[1] Instead, Pedraza was politely "invited" to leave the country by United States immigration authorities.

In midsummer of 1959 General Pedraza was also involved in an abortive plot, with the backing of the dictator of the Dominican Republic, the late Rafael Leonidas Trujillo, to overthrow the Castro regime.

Early in August, 1959, it was announced by *Revolución,* Castro's newspaper, that a plot had been discovered against the revolutionary government of Cuba, and thousands of men, formerly of Batista's army, were arrested. Prominent civilians who had been connected with the dictator's regime, as well as cattlemen and big landowners, were involved and many of them were arrested. For several days communications with the Isle of Pines and Las Villas Province were cut off by orders of the government, while rumors circulated widely about invasion and fighting in the mountains. Shortly thereafter the Cuban government announced that an arms-laden plane flown from the Dominican Republic had been captured, after landing in Trinidad.

It developed that anti-Castro elements operating from the Dominican Republic had contacted Majors Gutierrez Menoyo and William Morgan of Castro's army and had asked them to lead a movement against the government. Menoyo and Morgan promptly accepted but informed Castro. The exiles, completely taken in by Menoyo and Morgan, sent them a boatload of arms that was seized. Morgan and his men then went to the Escambray Mountains and pretended to be fighting Castro's troops. Later Morgan radioed to the

---

[1] General José Eleuterio Pedraza, a former high officer of the Cuban Army, despised by the Cuban people for the atrocities committed while he was chief of the National Police in 1935.

Dominican Republic and asked for a plane, which on arrival was captured. In the fight two of the invaders were killed and the remainder arrested.

It was rumored at the time that Major Morgan, who was known as "Henry" in this cloak-and-dagger game, collected $100,000 from the Dominican consul in Miami. According to reports, this infuriated Trujillo, who remarked, "that —— will pay dearly for this."

About a year later Morgan was arrested by the Castro police on charges of sending arms to anti-Castro rebels in the Sierra del Escambray. He was tried and sentenced by a kangaroo court and on March 11, 1961, was executed in the old La Cabaña fortress.

Even before Morgan's execution it was rumored throughout the Caribbean that a formal pact was in the making between the two dictators. Early in January, 1961—two months before Morgan's execution—Che Guevara referred to the Dominican tyrant in a speech as "our friend Trujillo." At about the same time the largest Dominican broadcasting station La Voz Dominicana, suddenly stopped its attack on Castro's Cuba. The other broadcasting station and all the government-controlled newspapers called off all criticism of Castro. Simultaneously the Cuban press and radio abandoned their propaganda against Trujillo.

Juan Orta, Castro's former private secretary who recently took asylum in the Venezuelan Embassy in Havana, told friends that the secret pact of nonaggression between Castro and the late dictator Trujillo was signed in October, 1960, and that the arrest and subsequent execution of Morgan was the price Fidel had to pay Trujillo for the pact.

Significantly, on May Day, 1961, when Fidel Castro formally declared Cuba to be a socialist republic, the Dominican radio went on the air with a claim that Trujillismo was the vanguard of socialism in the Americas. After Trujillo's assassination some officials of the Dominican government informed the Organization of American States fact-finding committee that a nonaggression pact between the two Caribbean dictators had been reached through a verbal agreement between Dominican secret service agents sent to Santiago de Cuba and Castro's military intelligence. However, following the death of the dictator this agreement was revoked by the Dominican government, anxious to patch up its problems with the Kennedy administration and the Organization of American States.

Another effort of the exiled Batistianos to get United States support against Castro was made when they proclaimed Francisco Cajigas as provisional president of Cuba. Cajigas had been a successful businessman in Cuba, had developed the Charco-Redondo Mine in Oriente Province, and had been associated with Batista himself in developing some business enterprises on the Isle of Pines. The Batista politicians thought that, since Cajigas had never participated in Cuban politics and was a businessmen, he would be acceptable to the well-to-do businessmen and landowners who were at that time the most important nucleus of opposition to Castro's regime both in Miami and inside Cuba. It was also their reasoning that his nonpolitical background would make him acceptable to the United States. Again they were unsuccessful in obtaining United States support.

As long as his only enemies were the old Batista henchmen, wealthy businessmen and landowners, Castro had little to worry about. It was quite another matter, however, when the discontent spread to the Roman Catholic Church and to those very people who had fought with him and helped him overthrow the dictatorship.

As early as the spring of 1959 defections began among people who had fought with Castro in the hills. The first defector of prominence was Major Díaz Lanz, commander in chief of Castro's air force. Díaz Lanz was a dedicated revolutionary and flew many dangerous missions to bring arms to Castro from the United States, Costa Rica, and other Central American countries. At the first sign of a communist take-over in the armed forces he defected; on June 29, 1959, he fled the country in a sailboat, with his wife, a brother, Sergio Díaz Brull, and a friend, Carlos Echegoyen. They landed at Fort Lauderdale, Florida.

Díaz Lanz charged that the Communists were conducting "a certain plan of indoctrination" in the armed forces and that "we all well know ... who [the Communists] they are and what aims they pursue."

These plans were afterward corroborated in his testimony before the United States Senate Internal Security Subcommittee on July 14, 1959. Díaz Lanz stated under oath that Castro himself is a Communist and that he had heard Castro remark: "I am going to introduce in Cuba a system like the Russians have, even better than the Russian system." [2]

Major Díaz Lanz also disclosed that from the very beginning of the Castro government there were Russian agents in Cuba. He mentioned the case of two Russians wearing uniforms of the Castro forces, who were arrested by the military authorities in Santiago de Cuba and later set free by Major Manuel Piñeiro, then in charge of Oriente Province. Major

[2] U.S. Senate Internal Security Subcommittee, *Communist Threat to the United States through the Caribbean*, Part 1 (1959), p. 6.

Piñeiro, known as Barbaroja (red beard), is now second-in-command of the dreaded G-2 (Castro's military intelligence).

Little credence was given by the Cuban people to Díaz Lanz's sensational disclosures before the Senate Internal Security Subcommittee. Fidel stated that Díaz Lanz was the "Benedict Arnold of the Cuban revolution" and that he was fired from the Cuban Air Force before his defection for "incompetence, extravagance, and nepotism." Castro was still very popular and few Cubans believed that he was a Communist or under communist influence. Even conservative Cubans dismissed lightly the serious charges made by Díaz Lanz against Fidel Castro.

Furthermore, some United States officials, including the ambassador to Cuba, Philip Bonsal, said that the Senate subcommittee did not represent the United States government. President Eisenhower stated that charges of communism against Premier Castro were not easy to prove and in the course of a press conference at the White House said, "The United States has made no such charge."

Many United States newspapermen sincerely thought that Díaz Lanz was the "Benedict Arnold of the Cuban revolution" and that his appearance before the Senate Internal Security Subcommittee was embarrassing to the United States government, which at the time was trying to negotiate with the Cuban government on the expropriation of United States property. Ralph McGill, a syndicated columnist, stated that "many responsible Cubans are saying that Díaz Lanz was a professional soldier of fortune engaged in flying arms to Castro for profit." In an article in the *New York Times*, Herbert Matthews said that the manner in which Washington managed Díaz Lanz's testimony "has aroused more bitterness and resentment against the United States than any event in the history of Cuban-American relations." [3]

Shortly after Díaz Lanz's defection, the defection of two Catholic priests—the Rev. Eduardo Aguirre and the Rev. Juan Ramón O'Farrill—again made it clear to thoughtful Cuban people that Castro was not sincere when he denounced anyone who opposed his growing entanglement with Communists as traitors and agents of American imperialism.

These two priests had fought the Batista government. Father O'Farrill had been arrested and beaten by Batista's secret police. Father Aguirre also was arrested and imprisoned under Batista's regime. Both had been forced into exile by the dictatorship. They returned to Cuba as soon as Castro took over and supported his government in its early stages, but due to their outspoken criticism of the communist infiltration in the labor movement they were harassed by Castro's police, and again left Cuba.

By the end of 1959, after the arrest and imprisonment of Major Hubert Matos, and the replacement of Dr. Felipe Pazos by Major Guevara as head of the Cuban National Bank, there were few noncommunist Cubans, even among the members of the Castro government, who did not see the handwriting on the wall.

As a consequence of these events, and the visit of Mikoyan to Cuba the following February, a frightening atmosphere developed throughout the island, and another exodus of noncommunist Cubans began. Thousands of people began to flee the country. This new group was composed mostly of professionals (physicians, lawyers, engineers, university professors, and teachers), small businessmen, labor leaders opposed

[3] "Cuba Has a One-Man Rule and Is Held to Be Non-Red," *New York Times,* July 16, 1959, p. 1.

to communist infiltration in their ranks, anti-Batista politicians, and even Castro officials.

Among the refugees who came to Florida in that spring of 1960 were some anti-Batista politicians of the Prío administration, including Dr. Manuel Antonio de Varona, former prime minister and president of the Senate, and Dr. Aureliano Sánchez Arango, who had held the posts of minister of education and minister of foreign relations.

Also arriving in Miami were young leaders from the Catholic ranks. One of them was the then relatively unknown Manuel Artime Buesa, a young lieutenant in his early twenties, who had served in Castro's army. He had also been an official in the National Institute of Agrarian Reform (INRA) in the early days of the Castro administration. He broke with Castro after attending a secret meeting of INRA in which Fidel laid out his plans for the communization of Cuba.

Another prominent Catholic leader who came to Miami that spring was Dr. José I. Rasco, a university professor and young leader of the new Christian Democrat party. Shortly after the fall of Batista, Rasco helped organize a political movement following the pattern of the democratic orientated Christian democratic parties of other Latin-American countries and Europe.

Many editors, publishers, and reporters fled Cuba when Castro took over practically all of the once free newspapers of the country. The first to arrive at Miami was Jorge Zayas, editor and publisher of *Avance,* the first newspaper seized by Castro. Following Mr. Zayas came José I. Rivero, a cousin of mine, and editor and publisher of *Diario de la Marina,* the second oldest newspaper in the Western Hemisphere, which had been published for 128 years. A few days after the seizure of *Diario de la Marina* the Castro government took over *Prensa Libre,* Cuba's largest mass circulation newspaper, which had been a strong advocate of freedom of the press and the right of dissent from government decisions. Sergio Carbo and Humberto Medrano, publisher and managing editor, respectively, were forced to flee to the United States. The only son of Carbo, Ulises, also fled to Florida. Ulises took part in the April 17 invasion and was one of the prisoners sent here by Castro to negotiate the "Tractors for Freedom" deal.

Italian-born Amadeo Barletta, who owned a $40 million empire that included the once independent newspaper *El Mundo,* several television channels, a General Motors agency, and a score of investments, was forced to seek asylum in the Italian Embassy in Havana. Barletta is now another refugee in the United States and his newspaper *El Mundo* is under the direction of Luis Gómez Wanguemert, an old leftist radio commentator of international affairs who has been reported as a long-standing secret member of the Soviet apparatus in Latin America.

Abel Maestre and his brother, Goar, who owned Cuba's leading radio and television network, are in exile in Miami. As in the case of the newspapers and magazines, all Cuba's TV and radio networks have been seized and are now operated under government control. Ironically, they are called FIEL, the Spanish abbreviation for Independent Front of Free Broadcasting Stations.

One of the most notable examples of how radio has been throttled in Castro's Cuba was the experience of Luis Conte Agüero, whose personal and political ties to Fidel Castro dated back to their student days. Conte Agüero took issue with the Castro administration over the question of communist infiltration in Cuba. At noon of March 25, 1960, he read an open letter to Premier Fidel Castro over Radio Progreso, urging him to maintain friendly relations with the United States and to beware the perfidy of the Russians, and warned that the Communists were taking over the revolution. He also expressed the fear that the only aim of the Communists was to make out of Cuba a sort of Hungary by forcing United States military intervention.

Immediately he was violently attacked by *Revolución,* and a few days later Castro appeared on television and denounced Conte Agüero in exceptionally strong terms. The next day Conte Agüero was prevented by a communist group from entering the radio studio for his daily commentary, and that night, after having been seriously threatened, he sought asylum in the Argentine Embassy, leaving Cuba shortly thereafter. Radio Progreso was, of course, taken over by the government and its owner, Manuel Fernández, was compelled to flee Cuba, joining the growing number of Cubans in exile in Miami.

Even Miguel Angel Quevedo, a stanch friend of Castro and editor of one of the leading Spanish-language magazines in the hemisphere, *Bohemia,* was forced to the conclusion that it was impossible to put out an honest publication in Cuba. When Quevedo took asylum in the Venezuelan Embassy on July 20, 1960, he explained the reason for his break with Castro:

The revolution has been betrayed, the republic vilely delivered to the nefarious interests of international communism. What many have justified as a political tactic to strengthen our sovereignty has resulted in nothing more than a diabolical plan, ably executed and progressively unfolded, to establish in the middle of the American continent a communist regime organized under the direction and close vigilance of Moscow.

Quevedo's break with Castro was described by Fidel himself as "one of the hard blows which the revolution has received." Today Quevedo and most of the staff of *Bohemia* are in New York publishing *Bohemia Libre*. The old *Bohemia* is still being published in Cuba under the direction of an ambitious former reporter of the magazine, Enrique de la Osa, who has become a close associate of Carlos Franqui, editor of Castro's *Revolución,* in spreading Castroite and communist propaganda all over Latin America.

The communist control of all media of communication has become so complete that even the notorious José Pardo Llada, known as the Goebbels of the Castro regime, whose vitriolic attacks on the United States over the Havana radio were a daily occurrence, recently fled to Mexico. From there he openly declared:

I am breaking with Fidel Castro upon reaching the conviction that in Cuba it is no longer possible to maintain a position that is not in accord with the line of the Popular Socialist (Communist) party and that any expression of independence, even in defense of the social program of the revolution is considered as deviationist, divisive, or counterrevolutionary.

The third wave of exiles began to arrive in the United States in the summer of 1960. They were of a different political background than those who came in the spring—who were predominantly representative of the right and center—and free of the Batista taint.

The new refugees had been closely associated with the Castro government and were unwilling to repudiate all that had been done in Cuba under the revolutionary government. They had fled Cuba solely because of communist infiltration and the delivery of the country to the Sino-Soviet bloc. With the exception of Dr. José Miró Cardona, Premier of Cuba during the first six weeks of Castro's rule, the new wave of refugees were noted as radicals and active supporters of the Castro revolution.

The most prominent of this latter group, Manuel Ray, organized the anti-Batista underground in Havana and served as Castro's minister of public works. A University of Utah engineering graduate who had become a successful contractor, he became a sabotage expert for Castro. In the first part of 1960 Ray again went underground, setting up his own clandestine organization known as the People's Revolutionary Movement (MRP) to fight the dictatorship. After several months inside Cuba he managed to evade Castro's police and escape to the United States.

Ray's MRP was not the only underground movement inside Cuba. Also operating were Artime's Movement of Revolutionary Recovery (MRR) and the University Students' Revolutionary Directorate (DEUR) under the leadership of Alberto Muller. The last group began its activities as early as Mikoyan's visit and strongly supported Conte Agüero in his stand against communist infiltration.

Another important group was the 30th of November Movement, an underground organization composed of anticommunist laborers, followers of David Salvador, formerly secretary-general of the Cuban Confederation of Workers, who broke with Castro on the communist issue. Salvador tried to escape from Cuba, but was caught and arrested and is now in prison.

These groups and Ray's underground apparatus gave Castro no rest in Havana, knocking out electric transformers, burning stores and warehouses, and sabotaging the water-supply system. Two hundred miles southwest of the capital, in south-central Cuba, the Escambray Mountains became, as they had in Batista's time, an important nucleus of guerrilla resistance. The Escambray, an area of precipitous hills pocketed with large caves and dominated by high peaks, is ideal country in which to hide. From May, 1960, when the first anticommunist defectors from Castro's army took refuge there, the guerrilla fighting forces swelled to almost a thousand men. But about a month before the invasion of April, 1961, the Escambray resistance collapsed. To deny the rebels a local food source, Castro had removed all peasants from the region and ringed it with more than 50,000 militiamen. All efforts to drop weapons, ammunition, medicine, and food failed. It was reported that the CIA was not very enthusiastic about establishing a lifeline of airdrops, and the fact is that by the spring of 1961 the Escambray resistance was finished.

Another growing nucleus of discontent was centered around those in the Catholic Church who were worried by the regime's ties with the Soviet bloc. Fidel was originally on very good terms with the Church, but as soon as he started his move toward communism the Catholic Church began to react.

The Archbishop of Santiago de Cuba, Msgr. Enrique Pérez Serantes, who had saved Fidel's life in 1953, issued a pastoral letter in June, 1960, warning that "the [Communist] enemy is within the gates." Msgr. Eduardo Boza Masvidal, auxiliary bishop of Havana, followed this up with a warning that "confiscation or arbitrary and unjustified expropriation is theft" and that "it is anti-Christian to stir up hatred and class struggle." Most recently Msgr. Evelio Díaz has complained of persecution of the Church in Cuba, and threatened to end all services on the island if religious freedom was not guaranteed.

Yet many priests and laymen did not believe that Castro's aims were communist and remained in favor of the revolutionary government. The most important Catholic fortnightly publication *La Quincena*, edited by the ardently pro-Castro Franciscan Father Ignacio Biain, continued to defend and justify every radical step taken by the Cuban government. With Father Biain were most of the left-wing Catholics and the militant Catholic Labor Youth (JOC). Even a Catholic pro-Castro organization, For the Cross and the Fatherland, was established to neutralize the effect of the growing anti-Castroism of the majority of the Catholics of Cuba, which represent more than 90 per cent of the population of the island.

Castro was rash in his reactions to the mild stand taken by the Church hierarchy and Catholic laymen. He went so far as to denounce the Roman Catholic hierarchy as waging a "systematic provocation" against the Cuban revolutionary government, which, according to him, was "instigated by United States monopolies and Franco agents." In a labor rally he called the priests "thugs in cassocks." Referring to Cardinal Spellman's statement asking for a day of prayer for peace and freedom in Cuba, Castro called Spellman the "Cardinal of the Pentagon, the Central Intelligence Agency, and the North American monopolists." The government-controlled press and radio stepped up their invective against the clergy, and frequently *Revolución* and other papers published small items, seemingly unimportant, but which in fact were designed as antireligious propaganda modeled on that of the Iron Curtain countries. "An American priest has raped a young girl" and "In such-and-such a religious institution the nuns teach young girls unnatural sexual practice, rendering them incapable of one day living a happy life" are examples.

With the growing antireligious campaign it became apparent that the Castro regime was determined to embark on a policy aimed at discrediting the Catholic Church in the eyes of the people. The Church reacted in a tolerant but firm manner. The hierarchy at last issued a pastoral letter to all its parishioners, denouncing "the increasing advance of communism in our country." The letter stated that the Church favored the social reforms of the revolution but let it be known that it would not tolerate a campaign of slander, and denied flatly any concomitance with the antirevolutionary elements. At the time this pastoral letter was read the Castro government had already embarked on a major propaganda drive aimed at linking the clergy with every act of sabotage and counterrevolutionary activity, and in some instances priests were directly blamed for individual acts of terrorism.

One of the principal concerns of the Catholic hierarchy was the growing indoctrination of the youth by the revolutionary government. Indoctrination, which actually meant brainwashing along the Sino-Soviet pattern, began as early as one month after Castro took power and for the first year, 1959, was limited to the armed forces. A Communist, and an intimate friend of both Fidel and Raúl Castro from their student days at Havana University, Alfredo Guevara (no kin to Che) was appointed to indoctrinate the illiterate bearded soldiers from the back country. The classes were compulsory, but they were not classes to teach men to read and write only—they were classes to teach Marxism. Well-known Cuban communists, among them the Negro poet, Nicolás Guillen, were often invited to La Cabaña Fortress to give lectures.

As early as the summer of 1960 it was clear that indoctrination had been extended to the public schools and that Fidel was determined to force indoctrination in Catholic private schools. "We will close the schools before we will accept such textbooks," declared a top-ranking Catholic educator in Havana. "We will not teach the Marxist interpretation of history and that would be the only interpretation permitted in textbooks authorized by this government."

There was, indeed, much reason to believe that the Castro government would welcome the padlocking of the Catholic schools. A major but little-publicized campaign for six months or more had been the planting of proper revolutionary thought in young minds. Fidel at times even toured grade schools to conduct a classroom dialogue in which he asked such questions as "Who sent airplanes to burn the sugar-cane fields?" "Where do invaders of the fatherland come from?" "Who wants Cuban children to be barefoot and without schools?" And the expected answer was always "The United States imperialists." Later in 1960 would be added to the latter, "Franco Spain and the fascist clergy."

Early in 1961, which was called the Year of Education, indoctrination became synonymous with education in all of Cuba. The interest of the indoctrination program is to brainwash the Cuban people to the extent of making them spies and informers for the regime. Cases have been reported of children making charges against their own parents as they did in Germany under Hitler.

Indoctrination is carried out under the banner of "alphabetization." Fidel has declared that in a year or so there will not be a single illiterate peasant in Cuba and has formed an Army of Education to go to the most remote regions of the island, such as the Sierra Maestra and the swampy

Zapata Peninsula, to teach the illiterate and make them good revolutionaries—which of course means good Communists.

The idea of a youthful Army of Education has caught the imagination of children and teen-agers and hundreds of them, from the sixth grade through high school, have jubilantly joined this army of teachers and indoctrinators, the number of which now amounts to almost one hundred thousand. In many cases these youngsters have joined against the will of their parents. The United States government is aware of this situation and has generously extended waiver priority to all youth whose parents want to send them out of Cuba.

Boys and girls chosen for the Army of Education are organized into uniformed brigades and given special courses of indoctrination which they will pass on to the peasant whom they are teaching to read and write. The Teacher's Manual has been prepared by known Communists and is said to constitute a masterpiece of Marxist indoctrination in the guise of nationalism and patriotism. It is almost certain that the peasant will be imbued with the Marxist outlook of the new society which Fidel Castro is creating.

Every possible medium is utilized to achieve complete indoctrination of the entire Cuban population. Everyone agrees that the indoctrination program is carried out with expertness and efficiency. With the government-operated radio, television and newspaper, with the thousands of Marxist books sold at low prices, with the control of all cultural and sports activities, and with the cutting off of the people from any contact with the United States and any other democratic country of the world, this campaign has been a tremendous success. Clearly Castro's efficient indoctrination methods were in part responsible for the Cuban people's failure to give their support to the recent invasion. Even the prisoners taken in that invasion have been indoctrinated by Castro personally. On his frequent visits to them he points out that the United States let them down in not giving them the support it had offered.

The Catholic Church foresaw the evil of indoctrination, and the march of events compelled it to an outright position against the Castro government. The first clash between the Catholic Church and the Castro regime occurred in December, 1960, when the militia and the Rebel Youth [4] began breaking up religious services. In some cases priests were arrested for questioning.

The Church reacted with an open letter addressed to the Prime Minister: "The texts for revolutionary indoctrination dealt with various historical and philosophical problems from an essentially Marxist point of view, and many professors entrusted with this revolutionary indoctrination took advantage of their conferences to openly defend communist ideas and to denigrate the doctrines and works of the Church." The letter also complained about the insults by the Castro newspapers and broadcasting stations against the bishops and Catholic institutions.

Referring to an attack on the Catholic university of Villanueva, administered by American Augustinian priests, the Episcopacy said, "Villanueva is not, as was affirmed the other day, 'a university of Yankilandia,' but a Catholic and Cuban university, a work of the Church whose professorial staff is formed almost entirely by Cubans, and whose foreign group is represented by a very small number of Augustinian fathers who did not come to this country to make money from their

---

[4] Rebel Youth is a merger of the 26th of July Movement and the Youth Section of the Popular Socialist (Communist) party of Cuba.

work, but to serve Cuba and to invest in it the money which had been donated to them in other countries."

The Cuban anti-Catholic drive, according to *Osservatore Romano*, the Vatican City daily, was Chinese in its origin. The paper pointed out that there had been circulated in Cuba and throughout Latin America a Spanish-language pamphlet published in Red China as a manual on waging an antireligious campaign. *Osservatore Romano* stated that the pamphlet, *The Catholic Church and Cuba*, was printed in Peiping in 1959 for the exclusive and confidential use of Communist party leaders in Latin America. The pamphlet warns Communists not to misjudge the power and attraction of the Church and proposes Communist China's establishment of a schismatic national Catholic Church "as an ideal way of destroying religion." It also warns against "making martyrs of the leaders of the counterrevolutionary activity of the Church."

The line of action to follow [the Red pamphlet says] is to instruct, educate, persuade, convince, and little by little to awaken the political conscience of Catholics, making them take part in study groups and political activities. By these means we must place the dialectic conflict in the bosom of religion.

Progressively we substitute the religious element with the Marxist element. Gradually we transform the false conscience into a true one in such a way that finally Catholics themselves destroy of their own free will the divine images which they themselves have created.

The pamphlet particularly stresses the need to destroy the supernatural character of the Church. Means for doing this are outlined as follows:

It is needful to establish a government office charged with overseeing religious affairs and organizations. Submission of the

Church to the centralistic democratic process prepares ... the way to patriotic steps which weaken the Church and degrade its image. This office will organize national, regional, and local associations. Each association must declare its faithfulness and observance of the laws of the nation.

"Moreover," the pamphlet continues, "ties between the local Church and the Pope must be broken. This can be accomplished by attacking those who favor union with the Vatican as unpatriotic," it says.

The pamphlet declares: "Thus the clergy is represented as being antipatriotic. The activists [Communist leaders] have the duty of convincing the masses that the individual can have his religion without the Vatican directing the affairs of the Church throughout the entire world."

Fidel Castro is following many of the directives of the pamphlet. The anti-Catholic campaign carefully refrains from attacking the Catholic Church itself. It is the "fascist priests in the pay of the imperialistic United States" who are the targets of this campaign, and it seems that the revolutionary government is seeking the support of the Cuban priests, who in Cuba number less than 25 per cent of the clergy. Of the estimated 700 priests in Cuba 550 are foreigners, most of them from Spain.

It has been reported that Fidel is considering the creation of a Cuban Church, divorced from Rome, but it is doubtful if it would meet with any response from the people, as only a minority of the practicing Cuban Catholics have followed the so-called For the Cross and the Fatherland, a pseudo-Catholic organization which supports the Castro regime. This organization frequently holds Masses and the few priests who participate in these religious rites are stanch supporters of the revolution. One such supporter is Father

Germán Lence, whose reputation is well known to informed Catholics. Father Lence attends and speaks at most of the mass meetings called by the government to support the revolution. He has been present at meetings at which Fidel Castro harshly attacked the Episcopacy for its open letter. "If the bishops excommunicate Father Lence they would have to excommunicate the government and the whole of the Cuban people," said Castro in one of his violent harangues against the hierarchy.

On Mother's Day, 1961, shortly after Fidel Castro's May Day order that all foreign-born priests must leave the country, the revolutionary government brought 10,000 peasant mothers to Havana to take part in the special celebrations dedicated to the "revolutionary mothers" of the new socialist Cuba, and a Mass sponsored by For the Cross and the Fatherland was held in the big Plaza Civica, where crowds of 200,000 or more attend Fidel's frequent rallies. The mass was officiated by the Rev. Guillermo Sardiñas, a major in the rebel army who had fought with Fidel for a year and a half in the Sierra Maestra. Major Sardiñas is the only priest who wears an olive-green cassock, the same color as the army uniform. He also wears the insignia of his rank on the shoulder of his cassock.

This Mass, which was broadcast over a nationwide radio and television network, took place only three weeks after hundreds of priests had been herded together in houses and public places converted into prisons during the April invasion of the Cuban exiles. Some of them were taken to La Cabaña, where thousands of political prisoners were being held. Cases were reported of priests being seriously humiliated, such as being interrogated while naked.

During the invasion jitters more than 150,000 people were

detained in Havana alone, and an estimated 250,000 to 300,000 throughout the island. All churches were searched for arms and it was reported that in many of them money and jewels were seized, of which only a small part was returned. In St. Francis Convent in Camagüey militiamen burst into the church and smashed the altar in their search for money and arms and in the little town of Soledad they even dug up graves looking for hidden gold. In the town of Jatibonico in Camagüey Province one priest was ordered to dig his own grave; soldiers forced him to kneel in it and told him they were going to execute him. It was also reported that there were mock weddings and dancing in some of the churches of Camagüey.

However, no priest was killed or wounded, and most of them were released, including Auxiliary Bishop Eduardo Boza Masvidal of Havana. Boza Masvidal is today one of the most popular figures in Cuba, and it has been reported through underground channels that he has even been applauded in the streets of Havana by opponents of the Castro regime. Boza Masvidal was actually arrested a few days before the exiles' attempt to liberate Cuba from Marxist rule. Havana's FIEL radio network reported that he had been arrested at the Church of Our Lady of Charity, where he was rector, because he was engaged in counterrevolutionary activity against Cuba, using his church for that purpose. It added that in Boza Masvidal's private office were found "great quantities of counterrevolutionary propaganda, two caps of the tyrannist army, one of which had a major's insignia, and also $236 in bills and considerable change in American money."

Five months later, on September 10, 1961, clashes developed between police and militiamen, and 4,000 anti-Castro

Catholics gathered in front of a Havana church to protest the government refusal to allow the traditional procession in honor of Cuba's patron saint, Our Lady of Charity. One youth was killed in the clashes.

The government radio and newspapers immediately charged that a priest had shot the youth and that the rioting was all the fault of counterrevolutionist Bishop Boza Masvidal, who was immediately thereafter shipped out to Spain with 45 other Cuban priests. Speaking at an awards ceremony, Castro said that in the future any priest, whether Cuban or foreign, accused of conspiring against the government would be deported to Franco Spain. "The fascist clergy," he declared, "is mounting a new attack against Cuba ... They are working with the U.S. State Department and the Central Intelligence Agency ... to plot internal disorders." Pope John XXIII publicly chided the Cuban government for expelling the clergymen. But Castro was not excommunicated as was former Argentine President Juan Perón when he began persecuting the Church.

All Catholic schools, hospitals, old people's homes, convents, land, and Villanueva University have been seized by the government. It is estimated that the total value of confiscated Catholic property amounts to more than $300 million. There is no doubt that in socialist Cuba the Church is beginning to go through the same humiliation and persecution as in all the Iron Curtain countries, although as yet Fidel has not called religion "the opiate of the people" and neither is there antireligious indoctrination as in the majority of the communist countries.

It is premature to predict what the end of this open clash between Catholicism and the Castro regime will be. In some Latin nations the opposition of the Catholic Church is enough to topple the government. This probably would not be the case in Cuba even if the hierarchy of the Church specifically condemned the regime and excommunicated Castro, who was raised as a Catholic and up to this time has not denied his Catholic affiliation. There are many reasons for this. As one Havana priest recently acknowledged, the country is nominally 90 per cent Catholic, although most of them are not "good" Catholics. They are, as this priest said, baptized in the church and usually buried in church cemeteries; but except for these two ceremonies, the Church plays only a limited role in the daily—and Sunday—life of the majority of the people. There were only about 700 priests in Cuba, or fewer than one for every 8,000 Catholics; in the United States there is a priest for every 160 Catholics.

The Church's greatest influence is among the middle and upper classes, those groups which were opposed to the Castro regime even before the anti-Church campaign began. Among Cuba's predominant peasant population, which is the main popular support of the Castro government, the influence of the Catholic Church is not so strong. This is perhaps the result of the shortage of priests, which in itself made it impossible to establish churches in the country or even to organize a system of religious instruction, such as Sunday schools for the children. In consequence, to most peasants religion is a curious mixture of Roman Catholicism and ancient African rites brought to Cuba by the slaves.

Despite this, the opposition of the Catholic Church to Castro should not be minimized. The Catholic Church does not own any land to speak of in Cuba nor does it have any political power in the government. Therefore, it cannot be associated in the people's minds with landowners and the corrupt governments of the past. Furthermore, Catholic organizations took part in the struggle against the Batista regime and many churches became sanctuaries for the persecuted. It would be very difficult, therefore, to represent the Church as a bulwark of reaction, as has been done effectively in other countries. Castro and his associates, including the Communists, know this, and it is perhaps their reason for trying to convince the people that the government's anger is directed against certain priests, and not against the Catholic Church itself.

A militant church opposition to Castro could have dangerous consequences to the Castro government, as it could provide a focal point for a badly fragmentated opposition. What is even more important, the Church could furnish moral justification to the fighting and killing in the struggle against the communist regime. Even before the open clash between Castro and the Church, the Catholic underground organizations were the most important. Most of the young men executed by Fidel's firing squads were members of the Catholic Student Revolutionary Directorate (Directorio Estudiantil Revolucionario). One of the members of this organization, Alberto Muller, is the nephew of Cardinal Manuel Arteaga, the head of the Catholic Church in Cuba.[5]

If Castro steps up his anti-Catholic drive, which is doubtful, it might force the Vatican to excommunicate him, as happened to former President Perón of Argentina, and which was a decisive factor in his downfall. If the Vatican should excommunicate Castro, it would weaken his position not only in Cuba but on the continent. In many Latin-American countries the Catholic Church is an important factor, and any open break between the Cuban government and the Vatican

[5] Muller was arrested and imprisoned, and it is said that Cardinal Arteaga took asylum in the Argentine Embassy during the days of the invasion.

could swing important support in the other Latin-American countries for sanctions against the Castro regime. At the same time the Catholic Church is almost as worried as the United States government about the inroads made by Castroism in the rest of the Latin-American countries.

Those who oppose Castro in and out of Cuba constitute a varied and loosely federated group. One measure of Castro's dictatorship and control is the ruthlessness and suppression he has imposed equally upon democrats and archconservatives, upon former supporters and former enemies, upon churchmen and laymen alike.

Thus the counterrevolution, which culminated in the unsuccessful invasion, is still in progress. Those who passionately desire Cuban freedom still hope for the time when the counterrevolution will take up the stated aims of the Castro revolution—and make them a reality instead of a ghastly travesty on democracy.

CHAPTER VIII

Journey to Disaster

I N THE spring of 1960, probably late in April or early in May, the Eisenhower administration decided to overthrow the Castro regime. The Cuban revolutionary government was moving steadily into the communist orbit. The U.S. Central Intelligence Agency had the information that a complete communist take-over was taking place in Cuba and that the Castro regime was a threat to the security of Latin America. There were reports that the Soviet Union intended to make a staging base out of Cuba for the communization of the other Latin-American countries and rumors that construction projects inside Cuba appeared to be designed for launching missiles.

Ambassador Bonsal had informed the State Department that all his overtures for a rapprochement with the Cuban government had failed. He stated that he was unable to see even Foreign Minister Raúl Roa and on many occasions he was received at the Cuban Ministry of Foreign Relations by minor officials.

When the "Castro must go" policy was decided upon, the Pentagon had plans for direct military intervention in Cuba, and it was said that former Vice-President Richard M. Nixon was the strongest proponent of this policy.

As early as April, 1959, as a result of a three-hour conversation he had in Washington with Castro, Mr. Nixon was of the opinion that it was necessary for the United States to overthrow the Castro regime. Fidel did not impress Nixon, and following this long conversation he wrote a three-page memorandum to President Eisenhower in which he expressed his personal impression of both Castro and the Cuban situation. Nixon believed that Castro, if not a Communist himself, was at least a captive of the Reds and a dangerous demagogue who posed a real threat to the United States.

A year later the Nixon memorandum was taken out of mothballs. The State Department had overcome its original benefit-of-the-doubt attitude toward Castro and was convinced that Cuba was being turned into a communist base for the subversion of Latin America. But direct military intervention was strongly opposed on the grounds that it would raise the cry of "Yankee imperialism." Also, under the charter of the Organization of American States the United States was pledged not to intervene. Article 15 of the charter declares: "No State or group of States has the right to intervene, directly or indirectly, for any reason whatever, in the internal affairs of any other State."

After some hesitation President Eisenhower ruled out the sending of the Marines into Cuba and decided that the Cubans themselves should overthrow the Castro regime. It need not be imagined that the administration had far to look for Cuban exiles to carry out this plan; plenty of exiles were perfectly satisfied with it, and displeased only with the delay. For months the Cuban exiles had been seeking United States support for every conceivable means of overthrowing Castro, including the arming and training of an invasion force.

The biggest problem was to find among the anti-Castro

factions, a group or a coalition of groups which the Cubans themselves would recognize as representing the ideals and aspirations of most of the people of Cuba and, at the same time, whose position would be pro-United States. Yet the task of selecting a Cuban exile group was not simple. It required considerable doing.

The anti-Castro Cubans were a gaggle of warring factions. They included Batista henchmen, officers of the former Cuban Army, archconservatives who wanted their land and money returned, discredited politicians, and left-wing reformers who wanted to preserve Castro's radical measures but without communism. There was no unity among them. The division was not only between the Batistianos and those who had opposed the Batista regime; there was also disunity within each group.

The Eisenhower administration entrusted the Central Intelligence Agency with the task of bringing together the anti-Castro exiles and training and arming them for the eventual invasion of Cuba. Richard M. Bissell, Jr., a former economics instructor at Yale, was appointed by Allen Dulles to coordinate the efforts of the Cuban exiles to overthrow Castro. It was recommended by both the State Department and some Cuban exiles that former Batista henchmen should have no part in the operation as Castro would like nothing better than to see Washington aligned with the Batistianos.

Yet the problem remained as to which Cuban group should get United States aid. The first choice fell to twenty-eight-year-old Captain Manuel Artime's Revolutionary Recovery Movement. Artime had been an officer in Castro's army and his group had been very active in the underground in Cuba against Castro. It was, however, a relatively small group and incapable of uniting the exiles into a cohesive one. After

long negotiations among the anti-Castro exiles with no Batista background, the Democratic Revolutionary Front was
formed in Mexico on June 22, 1960, and eventually became
the strongest anti-Castro unit. The Frente, as it became
known among the Cuban refugees, was the first successful
attempt to unite all anti-Castro exiles free of the Batista
taint. Much was made of the fact that the five exiles [1] com-
prising its board had all been anti-Batistianos, and two of
them, Manuel Artime and Justo Carrillo, had served in the
Castro administration.

The Frente seemed acceptable in every respect to the
United States. Its leadership was honest, its members were
strongly anticommunist; their ideals about a post-Castro Cuba
were democratic yet not reactionary. The Frente pledged
the re-establishment of Cuba's Constitution of 1940. This
constitution guarantees popularly elected government, with
the President and members of the Senate and House of Representatives chosen for four-year terms. It prohibits the seizure of private property except by judicial authority for a
justified cause of public utility or social interest, and only
after compensation in cash. It also prohibits abnormally
large landholdings, but envisages a land redistribution program with due compensation for original owners. It prohibits
the death penalty except for treason and espionage in time
of war. It prohibits solitary confinement, and finally, all Cubans are guaranteed freedom of speech and religion and the
right of peaceful assembly.

One of the most prominent leaders of the Frente, Dr.
Manuel A. de Varona, had declared that one of the first

[1] Manuel Antonio de Varona (Democratic Rescue Movement); José
Ignacio Rasco (Christian Democratic Movement); Manuel Artime (Revo-
lutionary Recovery Movement); Justo Carrillo (Montecristi Group); and
Aureliano Sánchez Arango (National Democratic Front).

measures of a post-Castro government would be immediately to restore individual liberties and return to American and Cuban owners the properties seized and confiscated by the Castro communist regime. He added that this did not include, however, the return of property seized by the Castro government from malefactors of the Batista tyranny nor would any farmer who has received title under the agrarian program be deprived of his land.

When the Frente was organized in Mexico it could have been considered as right of center in the spectrum of Cuban exile politics. Most of the refugees were still predominantly representative of the right, and the leftists had not yet arrived in large numbers. The Frente represented a coalition of groups whose views were perfectly in accord with the aims of the Eisenhower administration. They accepted the organization of a combat unit to overthrow Castro. As plans for a frontal invasion of Cuba took shape, CIA men went to Guatemala and arranged with Roberto Alejos, brother of Guatemala's ambassador to the United States, to use his coffee plantations, Helvetia and La Suiza, near the town of Retalhuleu, as camps to train an invasion army. A 5,000-ft. airstrip was constructed on one of these coffee plantations at a reported cost of about a million dollars, and beginning in September an airlift of U.S. planes shuttled between recruiting centers in Florida and the camps. Other camps were established in Florida and Louisiana for the training of Cuban exiles.

The entire preparation for the invasion of Cuba was conducted for months without anyone in the United States, outside of the highest official circles, having any inkling of what was afoot. But the training for a large-scale invasion cannot forever be kept hidden from the public view, and in any event arrangements for secrecy were not of the best. The Guatemalan airstrip was operated in full sight of travelers on the Pan American Highway and the Guatemalan Railroad, and in time the word began to get around. Leftist Guatemalans found out about the camps and a complaint was presented in the Guatemalan Congress early in October, 1960. The preparation for an invasion of Cuba was divulged in the Guatemalan paper *La Hora*, as early as October 30, 1960, and it was then described as "well under way." The alarm about the Guatemalan camps was first raised in the United States by a most unlikely source—the director and staff of the *Hispanic American Report*, published by the Institute of Hispanic American and Luso-Brazilian Studies at Stanford University.

While preparations for the invasion were being carried out at the Guatemalan bases, the CIA ran into difficulties with the Frente. The CIA found it difficult to deal with the five-man board and suggested the appointment of a coordinator-general. Up to that time each member of the board had an equal voice in a sort of collective leadership. At a meeting on September 27 the members of the Frente agreed to the CIA suggestion and appointed Varona as its coordinator-general.

The choice of Dr. Varona was clearly not unanimous. Immediately after the meeting Sánchez Arango resigned as a member of the board and pulled his organization out of the Frente. In a "confidential memorandum" Sánchez Arango charged "our allies" (the CIA) with manipulating the exile movement for their own ends. American agents, he said, were establishing a corrupt "bureaucracy in exile." He charged the agents had set up their own radio station on Swan Island in the Caribbean and were insisting that all communications with the underground in Cuba go through their channels.

Sánchez Arango now heads another splinter frente called Revolutionary Council for National Liberation, made up of many small groups which had been left out of the Frente or which had refused to come into the Revolutionary Council, set up in March of 1961 as a kind of provisional government of Cuba for the day when Castro would be overthrown.

Sánchez Arango was in his student days a Marxist, but in the late 1930's he repudiated communism and now is considered as being right of center in the political picture of the anti-Castro refugees. Although he fought the Batista regime, he had never associated himself with the Castro government, and he has strongly rejected the thesis of the "revolution betrayed" which is maintained by the anti-Castro left-wingers. Sánchez Arango thinks that the distinctions of left and right have lost their effectiveness in the struggle against the communist regime in Cuba. It has been rumored that recently he has been associating with officers of the old Cuban Army as well as with politicians who had cooperated with Batista, like the once powerful labor boss, Eusebio Mujal, former secretary-general of the Cuban Confederation of Workers.

Shortly after Sánchez Arango pulled out of the Frente the CIA was involved in another serious controversy among the Cuban exiles on two main issues: means for toppling the Castro regime and the ideological aims of the struggle to bring about a democratic Cuba.

In the early fall of 1960 Manolo Ray and other leaders of the MRP, the underground outfit organized inside Cuba by Ray during the summer, had arrived in the United States seeking coordination and U.S. aid for speeding up the fight against the Castro government. Most of his group had been Castro officials and represented the noncommunist wing of the 26th of July Movement. They believed in Fidel Castro's program of social reform under a democratic framework. They were not willing to repudiate all the radical reforms carried out by the Castro government, and the gist of the first manifesto of the MRP was: "To fight against the *'fidelismo-comunista'* faction is not to fight against the Revolution for which thousands of Cubans gave their lives, but to redeem it from those who have betrayed it."

The right and many of the center groups, predominantly those who wanted Cuba returned to its pre-Castro state, seemed quite disturbed by Ray's outlook on the Cuban situation. The rightists and some of the middle-of-the-roaders held the view that Fidel Castro and his close associates had never been anything but Communists and that the Cuban revolution was a communist undertaking from its early days. To them Ray and his associates were anathema.

Ray explained his whole philosophy to the New York *Post* in these words:

Our movement doesn't allow politicians to come in on the backs of the people just so they can get back into power and get money for themselves. We've had enough of that. What we want is a continuation of social reform—not a government by the rich or the exploiters. We believe in a mixed economy of private enterprise—because it is effective and efficient—and government ownership of utilities and monopolies—because these things belong to the whole people. And there must be freedom. This, Castro has destroyed.

Ray also held a different view on the strategy to be followed in bringing down the Castro regime. Ray and his MRP were against an invasion. They favored the slower "internal revolt" of the people through underground operations inside Cuba, and help, from abroad, for the guerrilla freedom fighters of the Escambray Mountains, who at the time were in desperate need of supplies and were completely encircled by more than 50,000 Castro militiamen.

Colonel Ramón Barquín, who had joined the MRP, was against any large-scale invasion, predicting that it would be disastrous if attempted. Barquín had also believed that it would be psychologically bad to sponsor what would inevitably appear to be a foreign-inspired invasion. He was in favor of infiltrating small groups and working from within.

The CIA was as strong in its objections to the MRP approach as the rightist Cuban refugees in Miami, who were calling Ray and his associates "covert communist agents of Fidel." The CIA agent appointed to deal with the Cuban refugees, Frank Bender, bluntly told Manolo Ray to join the Frente if he expected to get help. Ray refused and the MRP was not able to get even fifteen minutes of broadcasting time on the CIA-controlled radio station on Swan Island, a bit of deserted coral and sand off the coast of Honduras. Although CIA-controlled, the Swan Island transmitter was operated by a private commercial broadcasting station owned by the Gibraltar Steamship Company.

With the advent of the Kennedy administration the whole outlook for the MRP changed. Early in February of 1961, when the new administration decided to go ahead with the Cuban invasion, CIA agent Bender called representatives of the Frente and the MRP in Washington and told them to join forces and stop squabbling about politics.[2]

Shortly thereafter a pact was sealed between the Frente and the MRP in the Banquet Room of the Skyway Motel in Miami, and eventually the Cuban Revolutionary Council

2 *Time* magazine, "The Cuban Disaster," April 28, 1961, p. 22.

came into being as the supreme organ of the anti-Castro Cubans. Varona and Ray agreed on a three point program:

1. Top priority in the anti-Castro struggle should be assigned to help for the rebel forces inside Cuba.
2. Former supporters of General Batista should be eliminated from the training camps.
3. Command of the rebel forces outside Cuba should be put exclusively into the hands of the Council.

The distinguished lawyer and diplomat Miró Cardona, a man whose career has been based on mediation and compromise, was chosen to head the Revolutionary Council and to be provisional president of Cuba. On March 22, 1961, a provisional Cuban government dedicated to the overthrow of Fidel Castro was formally proclaimed at the Hotel Commodore, New York.

Only a few weeks after his appointment as chairman of the Cuban Revolutionary Council, Miró Cardona was informed by the CIA that the Kennedy administration had approved the plans to overthrow the Castro regime through an invasion by the Cuban Army of Liberation. *But he was not informed that the original invasion plans as drawn up by the Eisenhower administration had been basically modified.* The Eisenhower plan contemplated that the landing would be supported by an air cover to be provided by United States carrier-based jets. He was, however, informed that the invasion would be preceded by an air attack which would destroy Castro's air force on the ground.

After the invasion failure Dr. Varona, another of the Revolutionary Council's leaders, speaking in its name, categorically denied that the Council was informed that President Kennedy had basically altered the plans by refusing to let United States airplanes cover the landings. Varona's decision to speak out was prompted by Stewart Alsop's article in the *Saturday Evening Post* of June 24, 1961, "The Cuban Disaster: How it Happened."

While the Alsop story effectively bailed out President Kennedy on the invasion fiasco, it put the onus on the Cuban Revolutionary Council for going ahead with an emasculated version of the invasion plans.

Alsop wrote:

The next day [April 5] Kennedy called a meeting at his office attended by Rusk [Secretary of State], McNamara [Secretary of Defense] and Allen Dulles [head of the CIA]. At this meeting Kennedy made his decision to go ahead with the operation. But he ruled, under no circumstances whatever, would American forces become involved. Moreover, the Cuban leaders must be categorically warned in advance of this decision. Berle [Special State Department official] and Schlesinger [White House aide] were accordingly sent to New York to inform the Cuban leaders who unanimously opted to go ahead with the plan regardless.

The Council members, under fire from other Cuban leaders for their responsibility in the invasion disaster, concluded that Alsop's story was too much for them to take, and decided to break the silence and officially challenge it.

In a letter to Alsop, Varona said:

You incur ... error, due surely to inaccurate information, in stating that the Cuban Revolutionary leaders approved the invasion plans in spite of the fact that we were informed by Messrs. Berle and Schlesinger that the United States Government would not offer us the necessary military aid. ... That statement is against the truth; for which reason I find myself forced to declare that at no time were we advised that the Cuban patriots would lack the promised air and naval protection, nor were we informed of the date and place of the landing.

Varona concluded his letter by saying: "I leave to historians the delicate task of judging the facts and attributing the responsibilities."

I was not in the least surprised by Varona's statement, for I had already heard not only from him but from Miró Cardona, Justo Carrillo, and many other exiles that the Council was being completely ignored on the invasion scheme.

The major complaint was that the CIA never gave word to the underground in Cuba on the date of the invasion. The plans of the underground called for a concentrated campaign of sabotage, mainly in Havana's power plants, highways, and railroad hubs, to coincide with the landing. According to members of the Council, the underground learned of the invasion through the Castro-controlled Cuban radio, after many of its leaders had already been arrested by Castro's military intelligence agents. One of the first steps taken by Castro was the mass arrest of more than a hundred thousand Cubans suspected of being counterrevolutionaries while the landings were taking place. The only sign to the underground was a message from the Swan Island radio transmitter on the Honduran coast, which said:

Alert! Alert! Look well at the rainbow. The fish will rise very soon. Chico is in the house. Visit him. The sky is blue. Place notice in the tree. The tree is green and brown. The letters arrived well. The letters are white. The fish will not take much time to rise. The fish is red. Look well at the rainbow....

I was told by authoritative Cuban sources that the more than thirty-eight telegraph operators in Cuba who were in daily contact with CIA agents inside Cuba never received any warning of the invasion and did not know that the "fish and rainbow" message from Swan Island would be the signal for the uprising.

Despite the lack of coordination between the underground and the invasion forces, many Cubans still believe that the operation would have succeeded if it had been protected by United States air support as originally planned.

Yet the fact is that when President Kennedy took office last January he found on his desk in the White House an Eisenhower administration policy paper, known as the "Castro-must-go" paper, which ruled that the communist infection in Cuba must be eliminated and gave a detailed plan for doing it. The document called for an invasion of Cuba by Cuban exiles with United States air cover and logistic support. In fact the invasion had actually been scheduled to take place in November, 1960, but was called off by President Eisenhower when President-elect Kennedy declined to associate himself with the action.

The new President faced a grave choice. To call off the invasion scheme might have demoralized the anti-Castro exiles and opened the new administration to charges of appeasement. Kennedy himself, in his television debates with Nixon during the campaign, had advocated open aid to the non-Batista and anti-Castro rebels and complained that the Eisenhower administration was not doing enough about Castro. On the other hand, to back the exiles with massive United States air and naval forces would be widely regarded as old-fashioned Yankee imperialism. It would provoke resentment in Latin America, where, as Adlai Stevenson stated in the report on his recent South American ten-nation tour, the "principle of nonintervention is a religion." It might even provoke Soviet Russia to intervene and perhaps touch off World War III.

A spirited debate took place within the administration on what course to adopt between these two extremes. According to the Alsop article, President Kennedy had, from the beginning, strong doubts about the operation and was opposed to the direct participation of American armed forces in the venture. His military and civilian advisers were divided. While the CIA and the Pentagon favored the plan devised during the Eisenhower administration, the State Department and some key aides in the White House doubted the wisdom of an American-backed invasion. Secretary of State Dean Rusk was aware that the contemplated invasion would violate every "nonintervention" provision of the Charter of Bogotá. He pointed out that direct intervention or overt aid might mean that the United States would be accused of violating the United Nations Charter and Organization of American States treaties. Chester Bowles disliked the whole idea. Tad Szulc and James Reston, staff members of the *New York Times*, brought to light the CIA's plans to overthrow the Castro regime and raised many questions about the wisdom of the operation.

Despite his doubts, the President was persuaded to go ahead with the invasion plan. The information supplied by the CIA, backed up by naval intelligence, helped him make the final decision. Richard Bissell, CIA deputy director in charge of the Cuban operation, pleaded that it was "now or never." The Castro government was getting stronger every day. Soviet MIGs were arriving in Havana and by mid-May the 250 Cuban pilots being trained in Czechoslovakia would be ready for action. The President also was informed that the President of Guatemala was under heavy political pressure from left-wingers there to evict the Cuban exiles from their camps. The CIA insisted that Cuba was ripe for revolt against the Castro regime and that the Cuban Army of Liberation in Guatemala was at the peak of training and determination to fight.

On March 29, after making some changes in the plan, President Kennedy flashed the green light from the White House. One of the President's modifications banned United States air support of the invaders, which meant that if there was not a simultaneous mass uprising by the Cuban people the invasion was doomed to failure. The President also directed the Joint Chiefs of Staff to review the invasion plans in the light of the ban on American air support. The new plan called for air strikes on Castro's air bases to knock out his tiny air force. The air attacks were to be publicized as the work of defectors from the Castro air force but were actually to be carried out by B-26 bombers from Guatemalan bases, piloted by Cuban exiles. Miró Cardona was informed in New York about this plan by Schlesinger and Adolf A. Berle, Jr.,[3] but was not told that the President was substituting this plan for United States air support of the invaders.

On April 15, 1961, as was planned, three Cuban air bases were attacked by B-26 light bombers. One plane attacked Castro's main air base at San Antonio, built by the United States during World War II. The other plane worked over Havana's Camp Liberty, Fidel's main military headquarters. A similar B-26 raid took place on the military airport at Santiago de Cuba, 500 miles away in Oriente Province.

While the low-flying B-26 bombers were raiding three of Cuba's main air bases, Miró Cardona said in New York that the mission was known to the Revolutionary Council beforehand. "We have been in contact with, and have encour-

[3] A. A. Berle, Jr., former U.S. ambassador and assistant secretary of state, was Kennedy's Latin-American troubleshooter. He headed an interdepartmental task force to coordinate all policies and programs of concern to Latin America.

aged these brave pilots," said Miró Cardona. The pilots were Cubans, but not defecting members of Castro's air force.

The purpose of these air attacks, which preceded the landing in the Bay of Cochinos by a couple of days, was to destroy Castro's air force. But this purpose was only half fulfilled. A second B-26 strike was planned, which should have finished the job. San Julián, one of Cuba's best bases on the western end of the island, was scheduled for the second air attack, but the strike was canceled by President Kennedy as a result of Stevenson's protest that it would undermine his position in the United Nations.

The air strike came at the time when the United Nations had before it a Cuban charge that the United States was waging "undeclared war" against the Castro government. In the United Nations Raúl Roa, Cuba's foreign minister, accused the United States of staging the air strike. He said:

As further proof of the interventionist and aggressive attitude of the U.S. authorities, we have the fact that the simultaneous bombardment of these Cuban cities coincided with the appearance in the atmosphere of a large number of solar flares which make it impossible to carry out proper radio communications. This displays the high level of technical skill passed on to the traitors and mercenaries in the camps maintained in U.S. territory and in Guatemala, who are being trained by the Central Intelligence Agency. These are techniques that were employed during the Second World War for bombing objectives in broad daylight. Obviously, information from the technological and meteorological services of the U.S. forces had to be utilized to this end, so that the targets of the attack would be left practically without communications. The bombardment of various parts of the island began at 6 P.M. local time, just at the time when solar flares were recorded.[4]

[4] Roa, of Cuba, protesting the bombings of Cuban air bases at the United Nations, Saturday P.M., April 15, 1961.

Adlai Stevenson, U.S. ambassador to the United Nations, denied categorically that the United States bombed the Cuban airfield and cited the Cuban markings on one of the planes that had landed at the Miami International Airport with its engine nicked by bullets. But that night Stevenson threatened to resign and demanded that there be no more air attacks. The President then called off the strike which was to have taken place just before the landing.

It must be added that the cancellation of the second B-26 strike was only the last stage in the process of scaling down the Cuban invasion plan. Much earlier, even before President Kennedy's inauguration on January 20, 1961, influential liberals tried to scuttle any plans for an invasion of Cuba. Shortly after the elections Senator Mike Mansfield said that he hoped that President-elect Kennedy would be receptive "to every opportunity" for negotiations of U.S.-Cuban differences, and weeks later intelligence officers of the anti-Castro Cuban Democratic Revolutionary Front reported that Stevenson had been talking with Foreign Minister Raúl Roa at the Chilean Delegation to the United Nations in New York.

During the interregnum—before and after the Eisenhower administration broke diplomatic relations with Cuba—it was a matter of speculation in diplomatic quarters whether there would be any change in the United States policy toward the Castro regime by the incoming administration. It was known that there were many close to the President-elect who held the view that the new administration should make some conciliatory gesture toward Castro as the Cuban revolutionary regime blamed the diplomatic break on the Eisenhower administration. Argentine President Arturo Frondizi announced that any attempt by President-elect John F. Kennedy's incoming administration and Premier Fidel Castro's regime to negotiate their differences would be looked on with favor by Latin America.

The new President quickly ruled out any rapprochement with the Castro regime. In his first news conference, on January 25, President Kennedy said that the United States was not considering resuming diplomatic relations with the Castro government.

Yet the President soon found that there existed within his own administration many who opposed the American-backed invasion. Among them were some of his own aides in the White House, Walt W. Rostow, McGeorge Bundy, and Arthur M. Schlesinger, and more significantly the man President Kennedy almost made his secretary of state, J. William Fulbright, the Democratic senator from Arkansas who is chairman of the powerful Foreign Relations Committee. Fulbright made a passionate appeal, in what turned out to be a decisive top-level meeting in the State Department with President Kennedy presiding, opposing the entire operation against the Castro regime. Later the senator sent the President a careful and exhaustive memorandum expanding on his objections to the entire operation.

The CIA plan was also opposed by Manolo Ray's MRP. A story by Karl E. Meyer in the Washington *Post* of March 22 quoted an unnamed "prominent Cuban exile" as saying, "We can't fight Fidel and the CIA at the same time." Ray felt that the only way to overthrow Castro was to use Castro's own formula—to infiltrate Cuba with small guerrilla groups, to build up within the country a program of sabotage and resistance to the bursting point. So strongly did Ray feel about his plan to overthrow Castro that after the invasion he pulled his group out of the Cuban Revolutionary Council. It was

reported that Ray resolved to sever his ties with the Council
to protest the apparently continuing control of the CIA over
the anti-Castro forces in the United States and the small
support he was receiving for continued conspiratorial work
inside Cuba. Shortly after quitting the Council, Ray was removed as the MRP representative abroad by his own underground group in Cuba. It seemed that the MRP's underground
members in Cuba resented Ray's course of independent political action.

Much has been written about the failure of the Cuban
invasion. It has been said that the invasion fiasco was a tragedy of error and many people have been outspoken in plac-
ing the blame on the Central Intelligence Agency and the
Joint Chiefs of Staff. But the fact is that President Kennedy's
foreign policy advisers, anxious to protect the United States
from being posed as an aggressor, watered down the invasion
plans to a point that virtually doomed it from the start.

The plan to invade Cuba with a relatively small force of
1500 Cuban exiles was based on two assumptions: (1) control
of the air to secure a beachhead and (2) support of the invaders by the Cuban people as soon as a foothold had been
secured. These two prerequisites for success were severely
impaired when President Kennedy changed the Eisenhower
plan to give the invaders United States air support. The use
of United States air cover for the landing was discarded and
replaced by a plan for the destruction of Castro's air force on
the ground. This was the objective of the surprise dawn attack
on Castro's principal airfield on April 15, just a few days
before the invasion forces landed on the southern coast of
Cuba. However, this bombing wiped out only two thirds of
Castro's air force and the remaining third, which should have
been destroyed in the following air attack, gave a good ac-

count of itself in sinking the supply ships carrying vital ammunition and radio communications equipment, and afterward joining the heavy tanks in destroying the invading forces.

Much has been written about the failure of the Cuban people to support the invading army. One widespread theory held in Washington and in many other quarters was that the entire Cuban venture was based on a completely mistaken analysis of conditions in Cuba and the attitude of the Cuban people toward the Castro regime. However, both the CIA agents inside Cuba and the anti-Castro intelligence held the view that the Cuban people wanted nothing more than the opportunity to rise up in arms against the new dictatorship, and they confidently expected mass defections from Castro's armed forces and militia, as well as an uprising of the Cuban underground once the invaders landed. It was the view of both that the landing in force in Bahía de Cochinos would ignite a people's uprising throughout the island.

As the expected uprising of the Cuban people did not take place, and not even a bridge was blown up nor a railroad line destroyed to prevent Castro's military high command from bringing forces swiftly to the invasion beaches, the blame for the debacle was attributed to both the CIA and the refugee intelligence for their inaccurate appraisal of the real feeling of the Cuban people toward the Castro regime.

The fact is that the landing operation never reached a point where the Cuban people were confronted with a real choice between the Castro regime and the Revolutionary Council. The lack of coordination between the Revolutionary Council and the CIA on the invasion plans prevented getting word to the underground in time to put into operation plans of sabotage to block troop movements and create conditions favorable for an uprising. Just a week before the landing the head of the Cuban underground was smuggled out of Cuba and taken to New York for a session with the Revolutionary Council. He was supplied with two tons of powerful C-4 plastic explosive and ordered back to Cuba, but neither he nor any other underground leader was told that the date for the invasion had already been set.

Furthermore, the Revolutionary Council held a secret meeting on April 16, only one day before the invasion. At that meeting the Council was not told by the CIA when the landing would be made, or where. They were, however, flown to an abandoned air base somewhere in Florida and held incommunicado for the next three days, during which time the invasion had taken place. The reason for holding them was apparently to fly them to Cuba once a beachhead had been secured, on which they would establish themselves as the Cuban provisional government. It was their understanding that the United States and five Latin-American countries were committed to recognize them as a de facto government, after which Washington would give them material support openly through the Mutual Defense Assistance Pact.

On April 19 President Kennedy received a call from Dr. Miró Cardona requesting an urgent meeting. Miró Cardona and other members of the Council were flown to Washington in an Air Force plane and were received at the White House by President Kennedy. The prime purpose of Miró Cardona's trip was to ask the President for immediate United States military intervention to save the invasion forces from complete collapse. President Kennedy informed the Council that the operation had been a complete disaster, and promised that Cuba would not be abandoned. However, he refused to grant the Council's request for United States military intervention.

When the President decided that "in no circumstances" would United States armed forces be used to overthrow the Castro regime, Operation Pluto, as it was called by the Pentagon and the CIA, should have been canceled, or completely revised. The use of United States forces was the only factor that could absolutely insure success of an operation planned to liberate Cuba from outside with little use of the very forces inside the island that might have brought about a people's revolt—the underground and the guerrilla fighters.

Reviewing the chain of events in retrospect which led to the beachhead of death on the swampy southern coast of my country, knowing the bitter complaints and frustrations of many of the Cuban protagonists, and piecing together the real inside story of the invasion venture from talks with both U.S. officials and Cuban leaders, I could not help but come to the conclusion that the entire Cuban operation was a foolhardy military plan.

With a complete disregard for political, social and military realities, and an astonishing ignorance of subversion tactics, the CIA ignored the very forces inside Cuba that might have initiated a guerrilla-sabotage campaign throughout the country, creating chaos and confusion, eventually preventing Castro's deployment of his well-armed militia to head off the invasion.

For reasons unknown, perhaps fearing the overthrow of the Castro regime by the uncontrolled and somewhat leftist leaning forces inside the island, the CIA virtually allowed the Escambray freedom fighters to dry out before the invasion for lack of adequate aid from abroad—food, medicine and weapons. It should be emphasized that all the Cuban

exile groups, even the right-wingers who were the darlings
of the CIA, pleaded for full military support to the Escambray resistance. I shall never forget the constant efforts of
Dr. Varona in Washington to get help to the ill-armed but
effective guerrilla bands. Varona's brother-in-law, Ramón
Ruiz Sánchez, called "Commander Augusto" by the underground, was smuggled into the Escambray range to establish
better communications with the outside and a central drop
zone protected from Castro's militia. At the end of 1960,
supplies were finally parachuted to them by the CIA, but
most of them fell into the hands of Castro's militia. In short,
the Escambray operation was doomed long before the invasion.

The increasingly active underground was also ignored at
the time of the invasion. To some anti-Castro Cuban leaders
it seemed that the underground was not included in the
operational plans of the invasion. There is no doubt that the
CIA precipitated the invasion without adequate coordination
with the underground.

Many critics of the CIA believe the whole operation was
based on the assumption that a popular uprising against the
Castro regime would follow the first landing, and that once
the operation was underway, if there was not a quick uprising as expected and the invaders couldn't succeed on their
own, President Kennedy would reverse the ban on the use
of American armed forces and permit proper United States
air and naval cover to the Cuban invaders, even the landing
of the Marines.

Venturing further into the controversial role played by the
CIA it is a fact that the agency was at all times reluctant to
give help to the somewhat leftist Ray's People's Revolutionary Movement (MRP) and to all those that opposed their

plans. After the abortive invasion the *New York Times* disclosed that the most forward-looking of the anti-Castro groups, the MRP, "is reported to have received no financial support and almost no equipment."

The rightist leaning of the CIA was revealed also when the time came to select the commander-in-chief of the Cuban brigade. Of the many Cubans bidding for command of the revolutionary forces, some of them highly respected anti-Batista career army officers, the CIA chose Manuel Artime, who served with Castro in the Sierra but lacked the professional background of some of the Cuban army officers who had gone through courses in United States military institutions. Artime had become a leader of the right-wingers and the right wanted a man of its own in charge of the invasion forces.

It is quite possible that President Kennedy was not fully aware of these small but important details when he vetoed the use of United States armed forces and directed the Joint Chiefs of Staff to review the CIA's plans, logistics, weapons, and combat readiness to determine if the planned invasion stood a reasonable chance of success.

The CIA plans were approved by the Joint Chiefs of Staff, and submitted to the President, signed by the chairman, General Lyman L. Lemnitzer, and by the then Chief of Naval Operations, Admiral Arleigh Burke, an old foe of the Castro brothers. According to the report they submitted, Operation Pluto was "marginal," but did have a reasonable chance of success.

To many sources, the military judgment of the Joint Chiefs of Staff was faulty and the studies inadequate because they failed to emphasize to the President the risks and dangers of launching the invasion without adequate air cover. It was rumored at the time in Washington that neither the Joint Chiefs nor the CIA opposed the launching of the operation when the use of United States armed forces was ruled out, because they evidently took it for granted that once the invaders landed the President would authorize the use of American forces, even the landing of U.S. ground forces, if the operation went wrong. The last minute appeal of Bissell to the President to permit the use of jet planes from a nearby carrier to save the invasion was very significant.

There is no doubt that the unsuccessful attempt by anti-Castro forces to invade Cuba in April was lost in Washington. Most sources agree that the Cuban exiles fought well until their ammunition ran out and that the invasion was doomed by nonmilitary considerations. For the Kennedy administration the debacle on the southern shore of Cuba was a setback as grave as any that befell President Eisenhower during his entire eight years in office.

Far more important than these critical evaluations on the invasion failure is the question: what to do next about Cuba? Nothing in the Kennedy record or in the exigencies of world politics invites the belief that he will sit back and do nothing —or in any event gives that impression. As moderate and sensible a commentator as Roscoe Drummond counsels that "failure is tolerable" only if he "makes it clear that he is preparing to succeed."

CHAPTER IX

The United States and Castro's Cuba

NO ONE has any doubt that the cold war, with intensity and depth, has reached Cuba, a country only ninety miles from the United States. Even before the "American Suez" as the April invasion disaster is now being called all over the world, the Cuban revolutionary government represented a challenge as well as a peril to the United States in Latin America. The policies of Fidel Castro, after he became entangled with the Sino-Soviet bloc, threatened to open the doors of Latin America to Soviet intervention and to subvert the Monroe Doctrine. It cannot be doubted that such a policy represents a direct threat to the security of the United States and imperils vast United States economic holdings and United States prestige and influence in Latin America.

The repercussions of Castro's policies and his anti-United States tirades are felt even beyond Latin America. They are undermining the standing of the United States throughout the underdeveloped areas of the world where Castro's Cuba has become a praiseworthy example of a revolution against corruption and foreign economic exploitation.

It is obvious that this perilous and embarrassing situation is the result of old mistakes in the United States approach to Latin-American problems as a whole and to the lack of a realistic policy toward Cuba in the past decade. In dealing with the Latin-American dictatorships and the forces struggling against them the United States policy has been questionable and clumsy. In many cases the power and prestige of the United States have been committed on the side of a dictatorship repudiated by its people. In Venezuela, for example, the U.S. Order of Merit was awarded to Dictator Marcos Pérez Jiménez in 1954, over the better judgment of the United States State Department, and the United States ambassador saw fit to become an intimate friend of Pedro Estrada, head of the National Secret Police, a man as brutal as were Beria of the Soviet Union and Himmler in Nazi Germany.

The same circumstances hold true in the case of Cuba. The potentialities and implications of the Cuban revolution were not grasped by the United States ambassadors to Cuba, Mr. Arthur Gardner and Mr. Earl E. T. Smith, whose support of the Batista dictatorship contributed to the anti-United States state of mind of the Cuban people when Castro took over in 1959, making it easy for him to begin his attacks against Washington.

Neither Ambassador Gardner nor Ambassador Smith had had any previous experience in the foreign service, both having been businessmen appointed by President Eisenhower. Mr. Gardner was the United States ambassador to Cuba from 1953 to 1957, and devoted himself chiefly to exalting the Batista regime and to the promotion and advancement of United States commercial and financial interests in Cuba. He was so extravagant in his praise of Batista and his regime that at one time even Batista was embarrassed and remarked "I am glad that Ambassador Gardner approves of my government, but I wish he wouldn't talk so much about it."

Gardner's loyalty to Batista was thoroughly demonstrated on January 1, 1959, the day Batista fell, when he appeared at the Embassy in Washington with Nicolás Arroyo, then ambassador, and demanded that the leaders of the Cuban revolutionary group who had taken over in the name of the new Cuban government return the files to Mr. Arroyo. Gardner even went so far as to threaten Mr. Ernesto Betancourt, Castro's registered agent in Washington, that if the Embassy were not returned to Ambassador Arroyo, he would go to the police.

As to Mr. Gardner's business activities during the time he was ambassador to Cuba, it should be pointed out that he was especially devoted to the interests of the Cuban Telephone Company, a subsidiary of the International Telephone & Telegraph Company. The service of this American-owned telephone company was grossly inadequate, as any visitor to Havana can testify. The company had for years been holding off improvements while trying to get the government to agree to higher rates, without success. However, through his influence with Batista, Gardner managed to secure a big increase in telephone rates, and in gratitude the company gave Batista a solid gold telephone, which may now be seen in the Cuban Revolution Museum in Havana.

Gardner's successor, Earl E. T. Smith, made a very favorable impression on the Cuban people in the early days of his tenure. One incident especially stands out. A few days after he had presented his credentials to President Batista as United States ambassador to Cuba, he requested and obtained the consent of the Cuban government to fly to Santiago de Cuba to "get the feel" of the reported trouble between the Secret Police and members of Fidel Castro's 26th of July Movement. The day before Smith's arrival in Santi-

ago de Cuba, Mr. Frank Pais, a leader of the Castro underground and a brilliant educator, had been shot and killed by
the Cuban police as he was about to change his hideout from
one house to another.

As Ambassador Smith was en route to a meeting with the
mayor of Santiago de Cuba, a group of women dressed in
mourning gathered along the route carrying banners which
read "Stop Killing Our Sons"—a demonstration planned to
call Smith's attention to the brutal methods of the Batista
police. True to form, the police turned a fire hose on the
group to disperse them and manhandled them so roughly
that Ambassador Smith and his wife were horrified at the
brutality. Later that day he issued a statement criticizing the
employment of violence by the police.

Official reaction to Smith's statement was so strong that
some of the Batista senators introduced a resolution calling
on the government to declare him persona non grata. In
Washington, when asked for comment, John Foster Dulles
supported Smith for having issued a humane statement.

It is perhaps significant to recall that only a few months
after this incident Ambassador Smith, with Batista officials,
negotiated a substantial tax reduction for Freeport's subsidiary company in Cuba, the Moa Bay Mining Company.
From then on Smith's attitude toward the Cuban government changed. He accepted at face value most of Batista's
promises of civil liberty and free elections. His judgment as
to the true situation in Cuba was open to question.

Both Ambassadors Gardner and Smith appeared before a
Senate Internal Security Subcommittee, which has been
making a study of what it calls *Communist Threat to the
United States through the Caribbean.* In his testimony before
the subcommittee Mr. Gardner said that the State Depart-

ment "pulled the rug from under Batista." Gardner also said that the State Department "ignored him, and that no one would listen to his warnings about Castro." He disclosed that upon his return to the United States he had conversed with Secretary of State Herter, with Robert Murphy, Loy Henderson, and with Assistant Secretary of State Roy R. Rubottom, now ambassador to Argentina, and that he was amazed to discover that Murphy, top United States troubleshooter, seemed to have "an idea that Batista was a gorilla." Gardner made no bones about admitting that he was an intimate of Batista.

Although disagreeing with Gardner in many respects, Ambassador Smith insinuated that the State Department had contributed to the rise of Fidel Castro in Cuba. The burden of Ambassador Smith's testimony was that the United States government should not have established an embargo on all arms shipments to Cuba, as was done on March 14, 1958, since Batista was pro-United States while the Castro movement was anti-United States. In this connection he said:

Primarily I would say that when we refused to send arms to the Cuban Batista Government and also what I termed intervening by innuendo (which was persuading other friendly governments not to sell arms to Cuba) that these actions had a moral, psychological effect upon the Cuban armed forces which was demoralizing to the nth degree.

The reverse, it built up the morale of the revolutionary forces and obviously when we refused to sell arms to a friendly government, the existing government, the people of Cuba and the armed forces knew that the United States no longer would support Batista's government.

The embargo was, indeed, a blow to Batista. He had kept the loyalty of the Cuban armed forces by telling them that he had the unfailing backing of the United States government.

However, it was a sound step in the right direction by the Department of State and should be credited to those State Department officials like William A. Wieland, then head of the office handling Mexican and Caribbean affairs, who realized that the continued shipment of arms to Batista was creating deep resentment toward the United States in Cuba, as well as in the other Latin-American countries.

The feeling among the Latins that the United States is on the side of the tyrants and of the most reactionary forces gives profitable dividends to communist propaganda throughout the hemisphere. There is a degree of hostility toward Washington which has not been equaled since the days of the "Big Stick" and "Dollar Diplomacy."

Nevertheless, to accept the views of Ambassadors Smith and Gardner and those who compare the loss of Cuba to the "handing over of China to the Communists by the State Department," as stated in the fall of 1960 in a publication released by the Senate Internal Security Subcommittee, displays an utter disregard for the feeling of the Cuban people against Batista and of the sentiment then manifest in Latin America against dictators in general. At best it is very doubtful whether continued arms shipments by the United States would have saved the tottering Batista regime. Even Ambassador Smith admitted in his testimony before the subcommittee that "the Batista government was disintegrated from within" and "was overthrown because of corruption."

If a mistake was committed by the State Department it was not that of being opposed to giving military support to the Batista regime, but of being unable to persuade Secretary of State Dulles, and President Eisenhower himself, of the necessity for the United States to give every assistance possible to the democratic antidictatorial and anticommunist forces in the Cuban revolution that did not belong to the Castro movement. In this respect I am able to say that many officials in the State Department, particularly William A. Wieland and C. Allen Stewart, were aware that Fidel Castro was not fighting Batista to establish a democratic constitutional regime in Cuba. They were aware not only of Fidel's dubious background but also that Batista's regime was doomed, and that the only solution possible in Cuba was a military coup similar to the one that Barquín had unsuccessfully attempted in 1956. In this respect Manuel A. de Varona, Justo Carrillo, and others tried to persuade both the State Department and the Pentagon to encourage the Cuban Army to overthrow Batista and establish a junta composed of civilians and anti-Batista officers to take power and re-establish the Cuban Constitution of 1940, and to call for elections within a reasonable time. It was an approach to the Cuban problem along the lines taken by Venezuela and Argentina, where a junta took over and restored democratic constitutional government. Dr. Varona and Carlos Piad [1] tried through Wieland and other officials of the State Department to secure the support of the United States for a covert military operation to seize the Isle of Pines, where Colonel Barquín and many other anti-Batista officers were in prison. The plan contemplated was to free Barquín and all the political prisoners held by the Batista government on the Isle of Pines and to organize a base of operations against the Cuban mainland. This plan was supported by many antigovernment

[1] Carlos Piad represented former President Prío Socarrás in Washington during the fight against the Batista regime.

officers in Batista's army, and if carried out probably would
have succeeded.

A similar plan was elaborated in Caracas with the sanction
of President Larrazabal, who even promised the support of
the Venezuelan Air Force and some units of the navy. However, he stipulated one condition—that the United States government close its eyes to the operation. Justo Carrillo came to
Washington seeking the support of the American government,
and through Captain Jorge A. Perramón Spencer, former
air attaché of the Cuban Embassy, was introduced to Major
General Thomas E. Darcy, Western Hemisphere director of
the United States Air Force. Darcy was apparently sym-
pathetic to the plan, but after long conversations he informed
Carrillo and Perramón Spencer that the United States government felt the plan would create further serious tensions
in the Caribbean, and it was dropped. According to Cuban
sources, the plan had been discussed by the Joint Chiefs of
Staff and the National Security Council, and apparently was
not approved by the latter.

Although every proposal made by the Cuban exiles to topple the Batista regime and at the same time prevent Castro
from seizing power was rejected by the United States government for one reason or another, in the last few days of the
Batista regime an effort to force him to resign and establish
a caretaker junta which would be both anti-Batista and anti-
Castro was made by the former ambassador, William D.
Pawley. He made a secret flight to Havana on December 9,
1958, to urge his old friend—General Batista—to resign and
let the junta take over. Later, in testifying before the Internal Security Subcommittee, Mr. Pawley said he believed that
the only thing that caused his scheme to fail was the refusal
of Roy R. Rubottom, then assistant secretary of state, to let

him tell Batista that the United States government would back up the deal. Mr. Pawley added that the scheme was cooked up after a meeting in his Miami home with then Deputy Assistant Secretary of State Snow, former Assistant Secretary Henry Holland, and James C. King of the Central Intelligence Agency. "I told them that we should ... see if we can get Batista to capitulate to a caretaker government unfriendly to him but satisfactory to us, which we could immediately recognize and give military assistance to in order that Fidel Castro not come to power."

Although it is true that many United States officials, especially those in the State Department in charge of Cuban affairs, held the view that the United States should not commit itself to a corrupt dictatorship despised by the Cuban people, the fact is that Washington supported Batista as late as March, 1958, when the arms embargo was put into effect. And even after that many prominent officials, including the Pentagon and members of Congress, went out of their way to praise Batista and publicly to advocate military support of his regime.

An example of this was the awarding of the Legion of Merit to Colonel Carlos Tabernilla of the Cuban Air Force, who directed an air raid on Cienfuegos during the September, 1957, naval uprising. Another example was the visit to Havana in late 1957 of United States Marine Corps General Lemuel C. Shepherd, chairman of the Inter-American Defense Board, who publicly toasted Batista as "a great General and a great President."

As late as December, 1958, less than a month before Batista fell, Senator Allen J. Ellender of Louisiana held a press conference in the American Embassy at Havana, in which he urged the resumption of arms shipments to the Cuban government. Ellender said:

> Of course, I don't know much about it, but if a nation requires weapons to maintain internal security, I personally cannot understand why they should not be shipped. . . . People on the Washington level evidently feel that the shipment of weapons to the Cuban government under the circumstances might be picked up by Russia for propaganda purposes. But I do not think this is valid. It would be a tragedy for Cuba if civil war were to take place here. The poor people would be the ones to suffer. And Cuba is too prosperous and too wonderful a little island for such a thing to happen.

Ellender was not the only one to praise Batista in the declining days of his regime. On the night of October 30, 1958, the late Secretary of State John Foster Dulles and Mrs. Dulles were the guests of honor at a dinner in the Cuban Embassy given by Batista's ambassador to the United States, Nicolás Arroyo. Mr. Dulles toasted Batista, and the Havana newspapers headlined the event on the front pages. *Diario de la Marina* published a full page of pictures of the dinner in its rotogravure section. Dulles' attendance at an affair in the Cuban Embassy at a moment when his government was fully aware of the turmoil and struggle taking place in Cuba because of Batista's dictatorship caused much bitterness among the Cuban people, who regarded it as giving moral support to Batista at a time when his regime was beginning to crumble.

An incident of even more significance than the toast by Mr. Dulles was an all-out effort by the Pentagon to resume the shipment of arms to Batista. In a letter addressed to the Cuban General Staff, intercepted by Castro's secret agent at the Cuban Embassy, Sergeant Angel Saavedra, the military attaché of the Embassy, Colonel José A. Ferrer, reported that he had been informed by a four-star general and other high officers of the United States Army that the Pentagon and Ambassador Smith were trying to have the arms embargo lifted over the stubborn opposition of the State Department and members of the United States Congress such as Senator Wayne Morse and Congressman Charles O. Porter. The letter was made available to Ernesto Betancourt, registered representative of the 26th of July Movement in Washington, who in turn sent a photostatic copy by courier to Fidel Castro in the Sierra Maestra.

There were also several threats of direct military intervention in Cuba by the United States. When in June, 1958, Raúl Castro kidnaped thirty United States marines and sailors, seventeen American citizens, and three Canadians, Admiral Arleigh A. Burke, Chief of Naval Operations, wanted to intervene. Again in late November, when the water supply to Guantánamo Base was cut by Raúl Castro's men, intervention was considered. In both cases intervention was avoided by the Department of State.

After the water-supply incident, according to Carlos Piad, who participated in the negotiations, the State Department requested full guarantees from Castro that there would be no further interference. Following an argument with his brother Raúl, which was monitored by United States intelligence, Fidel gave full guarantees to the State Department and added that he wanted to be a "friend and not an enemy of the United States."

The whole United States policy toward the anti-Batista revolution was a zigzag one. While at times it advocated giving complete assistance to the dictatorship, there were instances when it appeared to be supporting the forces fight-

ing Batista's regime. The arms embargo, reluctantly accepted
by the Pentagon, was one such step. Yet, even after the embargo on arms shipments had been declared, rockets were
delivered to Batista's air force from Guantánamo Base. This
breach of the embargo was explained by the State Department as "merely a rectification of a mistake on an order that
had been initiated on March 2, 1956." In other words, according to the State Department, rockets that had been delivered to Batista before the embargo went into effect were
mechanically defective, and these new ones were merely
replacements.

Another incident which embittered the Cubans was the
rejection by the United States government of a request to
withdraw its military training mission from Cuba. In his
letter to President Eisenhower dated August 26, 1958, José
Miró Cardona, then in Miami representing all the anti-Batista forces in exile, asked that this military mission be withdrawn. In the same letter Miró Cardona pointed out that the
"missions would be withdrawn at any time and the agreement canceled whenever one of the two countries became
involved in domestic or foreign hostilities." He went on to
say:

It is well known and both your government and the Cuban
government have recognized it, that our country has been involved in a bloody civil war for almost two years. Nevertheless,
the corresponding Departments maintain those Missions in Cuba,
which produces deep resentment, since their maintenance, contrary to the spirit and the letter of the agreement, is proof of the
moral and material backing offered by the government of the
United States of America to the dictatorial regime in Cuba. The
North American Missions (army, navy and air force) are under
the direct orders of the Chief of Staff of the Cuban Army, by the

terms of the agreement, *and it is obvious that they train and support the armed forces of the dictatorship to kill Cubans and to fight against those who struggle to liberate the Fatherland.* [Italics mine. N.R.]

President Eisenhower never answered Miró Cardona's letter. It appeared that the Pentagon opposed the withdrawal of the mission, and on October 13, 1958, an answer from the State Department arrived. The reply explained that the "withdrawal of missions in case of civil war was permissive rather than mandatory" and that "hemispheric defense needs" required the United States to maintain its training mission in Cuba.

United States officers of the training mission remained in Cuba to the very end, and a few of them were on hand at Camp Columbia when Castro's victorious barbudos rode in to take over. I was there the day that the late Major Camilo Cienfuegos told one of the members of the mission that the "new Cuba has no need for a mission that was not able properly to train an army which disintegrated in the face of the enemy" (*sic*).

Given this record of United States assistance to the dictatorship, it is easy to understand the resentment of the Cuban people against the United States when Batista fled the country and the reason for Castro's tirades against Washington from the very beginning of his regime. "The tyranny unquestionably counted on the support of the United States. ... Batista managed to keep his troops in action for so long by telling them he had United States backing," Castro told his supporters en route to Havana for his triumphant entry into the capital. However, the alleged United States support of Batista is no justification for Castro's systematic campaign against Washington, for other Latin-American countries that have had more or less the same problems have not found it necessary to vilify the United States.

For example, President Betancourt of Venezuela, while in exile from his country, had grievances against the United States. Yet he is today one of the stanchest friends the United States has in the Western Hemisphere.

Since Castro came to power United States policy toward Cuba has been one of patience and the willingness at all times to negotiate its differences with the Cuban government. The United States was the first country to recognize the Castro government, just five days after Fidel had overthrown the harsh dictatorship of Batista, and in its formal note recognizing the new Cuban government the State Department said: "The Government of the United States expresses the sincere goodwill of the Government and people of the United States toward the new Government and the people of Cuba."

I expected, as did most Cubans, that a new era of friendship between Cuba and the United States had begun. Castro was widely acclaimed by the United States press, which, incidentally, supported him during his bitter struggle against the dictatorship. There were no criticisms of his announced social reforms, and one of the best United States career diplomats, Philip W. Bonsal, was appointed ambassador to the new government.

Unhappily the new period of good feeling soon began to fade. Within three weeks after taking power the new revolutionary government of Cuba had aroused criticism all over the world, including Latin America, for a series of drumhead trials and firing squad executions of former Batista henchmen. That April Castro let it be known that in the event of war between the United States and Russia Cuba would be neutral.

The uneasiness felt in Washington by the course on which Castro had embarked was assuaged somewhat that same month when in a persuasive talk before United States editors, and in visits with members of Congress in Washington, Fidel Castro defended his executions of the so-called war criminals of the Batista regime, implied that Cuba would support the Western powers in event of war with Russia, and called for a mutual understanding between Cuba and the United States. But in July of 1959 he accused the United States of "interfering" in Cuban affairs and before year's end began an intensive campaign of distortion, half-truths, and outright falsehoods against the United States government, its officials, and the people of the United States. Washington responded to these hostile attitudes and actions of the Castro government with patience and forbearance in the hope of avoiding a breach that would impair the friendship and mutual confidence which traditionally had existed between the two countries and their peoples.

This policy of restraint, or appeasement, failed completely. As early as October, 1959, Castro accused the United States of encouraging air raids over Cuba, and when Major Díaz Lanz, former chief of the Cuban Air Force, flew over Havana in an unarmed plane and dropped propaganda leaflets, Fidel had the insolence to charge that bombs were dropped. Moreover, a month later, after the United States government had expressed its regret for the Díaz Lanz incident, the Castro government and its propaganda agencies continued to foment the idea that Havana had been bombed. On May 31, 1960, Washington had to protest strongly, in a note, the dissemination in the United States by the Cuban Embassy and

Cuban Consulates in this country of a pamphlet entitled *Cuba Denounces before the World*. This pamphlet repeated the unfounded allegations that Havana had been bombed with explosives and strafed by two aircraft based in the United States and implied that the United States government countenanced these flights.

Coincident with the Díaz Lanz flight over Havana the Castro government challenged the United States right to maintain its base at Guantánamo Bay in Oriente Province, and in 1960 Castro charged that the Guantánamo Base was a link in a "counterrevolutionary plot." Castro propaganda began a campaign charging that the United States planned direct military intervention and that as a pretext the "imperialists" in the Pentagon intended a self-attack on Guantánamo Base.

Throughout 1960 relations went from bad to worse. The campaign of vilification increased; the seizure of American property without compensation was stepped up and in both the United Nations and the Organization of American States the Cuban government accused the United States of economic aggression. Even Ambassador Bonsal was accused of conspiring to bring down the Castro regime.

With the arrival of communist arms and technicians in Cuba during the spring of 1960, following Mikoyan's visit, the United States government abandoned the policy of patient restraint, a policy which had brought criticism to the Eisenhower regime in both the Pentagon and the Congress.

The first blow dealt Castro was in July, 1960, when President Eisenhower approved a bill drastically cutting the import quota of Cuba's principal crop, sugar. A month later the United States persuaded the San José conference of the OAS to approve a resolution condemning intervention by extracontinental powers in the Western Hemisphere; in October an embargo was placed on all exports to Cuba except medicines and foodstuffs. Castro's reply was the nationalization of 166 American-owned companies. This act, said the *New York Times* the next day, "virtually eliminated all investments of United States citizens in Cuba." The embargo was followed by the recall of Ambassador Bonsal.

The growing tension between the two countries reached a climax on January 4, 1961, when the United States broke diplomatic relations with Cuba. A statement by President Eisenhower said: "There is a limit to what the United States in self-respect can endure. That limit has now been reached."

There is no doubt that the Eisenhower policy toward Castro was one of patience and tolerance and that the State Department was eager to find a solution to the situation. From the time the Castro regime came to power on January 1, 1959, and this writing, the United States government has made nine formal and sixty informal offers of negotiation.

In note after note, and statement after statement, the Eisenhower administration indicated its sympathy with the social and economic objectives of the Cuban agrarian reform law under which United States holdings had been confiscated. It asked only that compensation be negotiated. Ambassador Bonsal went so far as to accept, in principle, a plan of the National Bank of Cuba to compensate for properties seized by the Castro government through a dollar fund which would be made up from loans furnished Cuba by international credit organizations and private banks. Castro was not anxious to go ahead with the plan, so he scuttled it by increasing his anti-United States tirades.

It should be borne in mind that many Castro officials were so eager for a rapprochement with the United States that they drew up plans which might have made it possible for the Cuban government to halt its leanings toward the Soviet bloc, keep Cuba within the inter-American system and on friendly terms with the United States. One of these was the plan drawn up by Felipe Pazos and José Antonio Guerra, when they headed the National Bank of Cuba, to make compensation for American properties seized under the agrarian reform law. Fidel never directly opposed these efforts of his aides. He let them go ahead with their plans, but when the time came to negotiate he always found an excuse to bitterly attack the United States, causing all these efforts to fail.

To all the United States overtures to negotiate the Castro government made only one official reply. That was on February 22, 1960, when the Cuban government announced that it would appoint a commission to begin negotiations in Washington at a time to be agreed on by both governments. Yet it attached one condition—that the United States must agree beforehand that during the course of the negotiations neither the President nor the Congress would adopt any measures which "might cause damage to the Cuban economy." By accepting this condition the United States would have been prevented from making any change in the Sugar Act, the extension of which was to be considered by Congress that spring.

Even after the Mikoyan visit to Cuba and after Castro had made it plain that his government was not bound by the 1947 Rio Treaty of mutual assistance, the United States government left the door open for negotiations. Since then, however, Washington has stated that it has no intention of taking the initiative in seeking bilateral negotiations with the Castro government. At the San José conference where a six-nation committee was established to investigate the factual basis for the charges made by the United States and Cuba in their disputes, Secretary of State Herter said that the United States would cooperate in every respect with the committee in finding a solution. On the other hand, the Castro government said that it would not permit a committee to come to Cuba to investigate the United States charges that Cuba was becoming a communist state and had associated itself with the Sino-Soviet bloc.

Even before the San José meeting the Eisenhower administration was not primarily concerned with the seizure of American properties in Cuba but rather with the intervention of the Soviet Union and Communist China in the affairs of the hemisphere and with Castro's determination to make out of his country a base for the export of communist propaganda and arms to the other Latin-American countries.

Following the San José conference the Eisenhower administration, and later the Kennedy administration, determined to topple the Castro regime because both administrations realized that the United States defense perimeter, formerly on the other side of the great oceans, has been bridged and a hostile base established within 90 miles of its shores. The communist regime in Cuba is a military threat to the United States, endangers United States communications in the Caribbean, and provides a springboard for the extension of the communist system to all Latin America. It was to avert precisely such a situation that the Monroe Doctrine was proclaimed in the nineteenth century, and it was precisely for this reason that the Kennedy administration approved, although with modifications, the Eisenhower plan to overthrow the Castro regime through the invasion by Cuban exiles.

The debacle of the April invasion has put the United States in a very difficult position. Its prestige, heavily involved in "the Cuban episode," as President Kennedy called the Cuban invasion, suffered a major blow all over the world. The fiasco had repercussions not only in Latin America but also among European allies and Asian neutrals. Castro himself claimed a major victory—not only in the struggle with the Cuban anti-Communists at home but in his propaganda war against the United States throughout the world. The United States faced not only the important problem of Cuba but the larger problem of conducting cold war operations. The dilemma is this: any new direct military intervention by the United States in Cuba would weaken Washington's position in its struggle with Russia to win the noncommitted nations of the world. At the same time a policy of restraint in dealing with the Castro regime could mean in the long run the communization of all Latin America.

CHAPTER X

What Could Be Done?

CUBA has become a focus of grave international tension. Soviet Russia has threatened the United States itself if Washington intervened in Cuba. A report widespread in Washington during the April invasion of Cuba by anti-Castro Cubans was that President Kennedy received a secret note from Khrushchev, stating that if U.S. forces intervened East German troops would move into West Berlin.

On the other hand, Castro's efforts at land reform and his expropriation of foreign holdings are striking a responsive chord among the dispossessed of this hemisphere. To them, fears of communist infiltration are decidedly secondary. Latin-American leaders are conscious of the pro-Castro sentiment among their people; many fear to take too strong a public position on Cuba lest they touch off an explosion inside their own country. This is the hard fact behind the appeasement of the Castro regime by a number of Latin-American governments.

The problem now facing President Kennedy on Cuba is indeed a most difficult one. Any course of action is risky and might even involve the United States in a war with Russia. Broadly speaking, the big question faced by the Kennedy administration is how to put a stop to the Soviet buildup in

Cuba and to communist infiltration in the Western Hemisphere.

After the Cuban invasion failure President Kennedy, in a speech before the American Society of Newspaper Editors in Washington, said that the United States will not indefinitely tolerate in the Americas a communist dictatorship subject to foreign control. Here are his words:

Should it ever appear that the inter-American doctrine of non-interference merely conceals or excuses a policy of nonaction—if the nations of this hemisphere should fail to meet their commitments against outside communist penetration—then I want it clearly understood that this government will not hesitate in meeting its primary obligations, which are to the security of our own nation.

The President further declared: "Cuba must not be abandoned to the Communists. And we do not intend to abandon it either."

The day before this address President Kennedy had conferred in the White House with Dr. José Miró Cardona and the other members of the Cuban Revolutionary Council and assured them that the United States will take the necessary steps to rescue Cuba.

Since the failure of the attempt to overthrow the Castro regime the United States has been realigning its own policy toward Cuba. The administration has been consulting Latin-American governments on some joint action under the hemisphere's collective-security arrangements. The bases for collective action against the Castro dictatorship are provided in both the Rio Treaty of 1947 and the Caracas Resolution in 1954.

Article VI of the Rio Treaty (Inter-American Treaty of Reciprocal Assistance) reads as follows:

If the inviolability or the integrity of the territory or the sovereignty or political independence of any American state should be affected by an aggression which is not an armed attack or by an extra-continental or intra-continental conflict, or by any other fact or situation that might endanger the peace of America [the foreign ministers of the member states] shall meet immediately in order to agree on the measures which must be taken in case of aggression to assist the victim of the aggression or, in any case, the measures which should be taken for the common defense and for the maintenance of the peace and security of the continent.

The defensive measures to be taken are enumerated in Article VIII, and include the use of armed forces. Such collective action is defined by the very charter of the Organization of American States as not being a violation of the principles of nonintervention (Article 19).

By the Anti-Communist Resolution of Caracas, adopted in 1954, all the American republics are bound to act collectively against "the domination or control of the political institutions of any American States by the international Communist movement, extending to this Hemisphere the political system of an extra-continental power."

In the documents submitted by former Secretary of State Christian A. Herter to the Latin-American foreign ministers at San José, Costa Rica, in 1960, the United States made clear its conviction that the Castro government was "walking hand-in-hand" with the Sino-Soviet bloc, and that this endangered the peace and security of the Western Hemisphere. But Secretary Herter refrained from invoking either of the inter-American obligations—the Rio Treaty or the Caracas Resolution—because he was aware that many of the foreign ministers, including the Peruvian whose government had called for the meeting, were reluctant to side with the United States against the Castro government. The Latin-

American states condemned the Sino-Soviet intervention in the hemisphere but significantly refused to criticize Cuba by name. A probable interpretation of the watered-down resolution finally adopted at San José appears to be that many Latin-American governments, always touchy about their sovereignty, are reluctant to participate in any joint action which can be described as "intervention in the internal affairs of another American state." Furthermore, communism has a very real appeal to many of Latin America's poor. Castro's agrarian reform has wide popular support and the dictatorial aspects of his regime have little impact on people long ruled by right-wing dictatorships.

Adlai Stevenson's report on his ten-nation tour in South America, as far as Cuba is concerned, was really frightening. He encountered a widespread tendency to see Cuba as a problem in United States-Cuban relations rather than a hemispheric one. Even more disturbing, he saw clearly that the imagination of the people has been captured by the Castro revolution. The difficulty of fighting a captivating idea is obvious. Castroism could easily become a rallying cry for more revolutions of the same pattern. Stevenson reported that the reluctance of the Latin-American leaders to side with the United States is due largely to their awareness of this sentiment among a large segment of the populace.

On the other hand, he found considerable enthusiasm for the idea behind President Kennedy's Alliance for Progress, which appears to be the prescription of the liberal wing of the administration effectively to counter Castro's communist subversion. A viewpoint commonly heard today is that the only answer to the spread of communist Castroism throughout Latin America lies in social and economic reforms heavily buttressed by United States economic aid.

Stevenson's appraisal of the Latin-American situation was absolutely accurate. The hemispheric economic meeting at Punta del Este, Uruguay, in August, 1961, demonstrated that there was a great enthusiasm for the Alliance for Progress program but that there was still no chance of lining up the major Latin-American nations against the Castro regime.

The Punta del Este conference was not called to deal with Castro's attempts at subversion, but Cuba's chief delegate, Che Guevara, provided most of the color and drama at the Alliance for Progress meeting. By charming his fellow Latin-American delegates, the intelligent Argentine-Cuban leader managed to gain support from some of the key Latin-American governments, like Argentina, Brazil, Chile and Mexico, for an accommodation with the United States. Following the meeting, Guevara held private talks with both President Arturo Frondizi of Argentina and President Quadros of Brazil.

According to well-informed Latin-American diplomats and other observers, Guevara told both Frondizi and Quadros that the United States economic boycott was causing serious economic problems. The Argentine newspaper *Correo de la Tarde* said that the Cuban government is being pushed by economic distress to seek a reconciliation with the United States. It added that President Frondizi reported to the chiefs of the Argentine armed forces that Guevara told him Cuba would not become a member of the Warsaw Pact and that Castro was anxious for a reconciliation with Washington.

The United States was skeptical about the new Cuban interest in a rapprochement. It remains the Washington position that normal relations with Cuba are out of the question as long as a communist regime remains in power in Havana.

At the end of the Punta del Este conference, Secretary of the Treasury Dillon put an end to the rumors that a reconciliation between the United States and Cuba might be possible. Cuba would not receive a cent from the alliance, Dillon said, "as long as [it] remains under the control of a foreign power—namely, the Soviet Union."

If the Castro regime was not a dynamic communist dictatorship, dedicated to spreading its influence to the other Latin-American countries, a fact which is generally admitted, President Kennedy's Alliance for Progress would be the most effective weapon to blunt the Castro challenge. Castro has undoubtedly an extensive following among the impoverished Latin-American masses. The Alliance for Progress program is directed toward the complex problem of raising per capita productivity and the redistribution of wealth so as to enable peoples long exploited or grievously neglected to attain a humanly decent way of life.

Unfortunately, the Alliance for Progress is a long-range program. It is going to take some time before the multibillion, ambitious, and expensive program can bring about any real improvement in the conditions which now make the Castro revolution attractive to the underprivileged classes of Latin America.

On the other hand, Castro is sincerely convinced that Marxism is the way of the future and that it is only a question of time until social revolutions of the Cuban type will spread throughout Latin America. He is also convinced that the Alliance for Progress will not work because it does not affect the out-of-date social structure of the Latin-American countries, which is the cause of the conditions that President Kennedy's program wants to alleviate.

This, however, is not true. The Alliance for Progress is in

itself a slow but a real revolution. A minimum of $20 billion in foreign aid is pledged for Latin America in the next decade. More than half will come from the United States (some in low-interest, long-term loans), the rest from international credit agencies (Inter-American Development Bank, International Bank for Reconstruction and Development, and the International Monetary Fund), Western Europe, and private capital.

As important as the money offered was President Kennedy's insistence—written into the final agreement signed at Punta del Este—that the beneficiaries must undertake massive and long-needed social reform to qualify. This means that Latins have pledged themselves to two basic—and controversial—structural reforms. One is agrarian reform, distributing large landholdings now in the hands of a small feudal minority. The other is tax reform—"redistributing the national income in order to benefit those who are most in need."

These reforms might be the solution to Latin America's widespread illiteracy, its historic economic and political instability, its lack of experience with industrialization, and other problems of underdeveloped economies. Surely Castro and the Communists will step up their troublemaking in an attempt to sabotage the Alliance for Progress. Castro is willingly tied to a hemispheric conspiracy which serves the purpose of the Soviet Union to dominate those Latin-American countries which are ripe for revolutionary changes. He will not stop at stirring up riots and provoking situations of unrest to hamper a program of economic development.

The success of the Alliance for Progress is closely related to a climate of economic confidence, unattainable while Castro continues to agitate and to push his revolution. Since

Castro began socializing the Cuban economy, Latin-American capital has fled to Europe in astronomical amounts. Estimates differ on how much capital has moved, but it has been reported by banking circles that more than $2 billion has been taken out of the Latin-American countries. When Castro's communist riots shook Caracas in 1960, bankers ascertained that $300 million in Venezuelan capital took flight. The first precautionary step of the Latin-American upper classes was to open numbered accounts in Swiss banks.

It is difficult to see how President Kennedy's Alliance for Progress would benefit the masses of Latin America—even if Congress responds to the administration's request for large sums—if there is not in Latin America a proper atmosphere for private investment and peaceful development of the region. According to the Department of Commerce, United States business and individual investments in Latin America fell from $216 million in 1959 to $95 million in 1960, at a time when U.S. investments abroad were generally increasing. The Commerce Department attributed the general decline to the "low level of activity in the petroleum industry" and to the "situation in Cuba."

If the Castro regime is allowed to continue for any further measurable length of time as the spearhead of communist penetration into the other Latin-American republics, the Alliance for Progress will be doomed. The Western Hemisphere will then be in dire peril of communist conquest, not only by espionage, subversion, infiltration, or even armed aggression but by economic stagnation.

Faced with this almost impossible dilemma, the Kennedy administration has several different courses open to it. Each has its disadvantages, its advantages, and its inevitable risks:

1. *The hands-off policy.* It is difficult to see how the

United States could follow a complete hands-off policy toward the Castro regime. In the event of such a decision the United States would eventually lose all its influence in Latin America and its prestige in the United Nations and in the world at large. For most of the Latins the image of the United States would be that of a decadent nation with no power to defend its own political, economic, and military interests.

The result would be that most of the present governments of Latin America would either follow a neutralist policy in the cold war or would be replaced or overthrown by those in favor of a government of the Castro sort. In the long run it would mean the possible withdrawal of the United States from the underprivileged areas of the world, leaving Asia and Africa open to communist infiltration and dominance.

On the other hand, it will be argued by those in favor of a hands-off policy that the Castro regime would eventually collapse by its incapacity to solve its pressing economic problems, and it is doubtful if the Soviet bloc of nations would be in a position to grant Cuba the necessary aid. A communist Cuba, in economic misery, would be a living example to the rest of Latin America of what would be in store for them should Castro communism eventually prevail in their own countries.

All these arguments for a hands-off policy toward Cuba might be plausible if it were not for the fact that Cuba is a country relatively rich in resources, with good communications, and without the drawback of great masses of illiterate people not yet incorporated into a civilized society, as is the case with many of the other Latin-American countries. The United States cannot assume that the Soviet will allow Cuba to be an economic failure. On the contrary, it can be assumed that the Soviet bloc of nations will do everything in its power to transform Cuba into a shining example of a prosperous communist state.

2. *Appeasement.* This approach would not be workable. Appeasement would mean United States concessions to Castro, negotiations for the re-establishment of diplomatic relations, and the acceptance by Washington of a communist state on its doorstep. Castro might be willing to reach an agreement with the United States even without the re-establishment of the Cuban sugar quota or economic aid from the Alliance for Progress. He and his associates would like nothing better than a breathing spell to reorganize the country's shattered economy on a communist basis. Most Cuban Communists hope that the United States realizes that Cuba is a "lost cause." They are convinced that the future of the world is communist and that it is only a matter of time before this dream is realized. When I was in the Cuban Foreign Office I was impressed by the fact that all the Communists feared direct military intervention by the United States, because they were convinced that the United States, under its present capitalist system and its far-flung international commitments, could not permit the Castro regime to survive. However, most of them thought that in case the United States failed to act and the Cuban revolution survived, say, for another two years, it would stand as an example to all Latin America that the "imperialists" could be defied, and then nothing could prevent their communization.

Hypothetically, if the decision in Washington were for appeasement, Castro would request that the United States withdraw support from all Cuban exiles and take no steps that might be interpreted in Latin America as being hostile to his regime. But even if the United States made concessions, including economic and technical aid to Cuba, it is doubtful that Castro would make any move without the consent of the Soviet Union. If Russia agreed, Castro might accept some conditions from the Kennedy administration that would be acceptable to the United States public. Those concessions might be the stopping of the firing squad executions, and the celebration of elections in the communist pattern, and a restraint on his anti-United States tirades. But Castro would never accept a change in his present policy toward the complete integration of Cuba's political and economic system with the communist bloc of nations.

According to Latin-American diplomats who explored Che Guevara's views in depth at the Punta del Este meeting, Cuba will have elections but there will be only one party, the newly created "United Party of the Socialist Revolution," of which Fidel Castro would be secretary-general. Guevara said—according to these diplomats—that the Cuban revolution needed a centralization of political decision and that this could not be achieved through a multiparty system, which is a Marxist-Leninist concept of democracy.

Moreover, Castro believes, according to Tad Szulc of the *New York Times* who spoke with him after the April invasion, that the Cuban revolution can no longer be overthrown by the United States and that he is the chosen instrument to bring about the collapse of capitalism and imperialism.

In other words, any concessions that the United States might make Castro would not lead him to abandon his revolutionary ideas of becoming the Lenin of Latin America. So confident is Castro in the ultimate victory of Marxism in the world that he has no hesitation in telling any American visitors that the United States is doomed as the last bulwark of capitalism.

It is inconceivable, therefore, that anyone could advocate a policy of appeasement as a solution to the grave problem which the Castro regime poses for the United States and the other American republics.

3. *Containment.* Another approach is the so-called policy of containment, which means an all-out joint effort with the Latin-American republics to isolate the Castro regime to prevent its ideological expansion in Latin America through propaganda, infiltration, and subversion, if not by actual armed aggression.

The United States policy for Cuba appeared to be—after the April invasion—to prevent the spread of Castro communism to other countries. For some weeks the State Department consulted Latin Americans on the prospects for a special OAS foreign ministers' meeting on Cuba and attempted to achieve an advance agreement on what to do. It was reported that the most important and likely step under consideration was to revive the hemispheric Political Defense Committee, which fought Nazi sabotage and infiltration in World War II, this time to combat communist and Castroist subversion. At this writing, a conference along these lines has been arranged. With the United States taking the lead, 14 of the organization's 21 members voted, on December 4, 1961, in favor of holding a foreign ministers conference in January, 1962. Mexico joined Communist Cuba in opposing the meeting, while Argentina, Bolivia, Brazil, Chile and Ecuador abstained. However, the United States was able to coalesce the two-thirds majority that will be required for future political or military sanctions against the Castro regime. There is no doubt that, if the United States can be assured of getting more than two-thirds support, it will ask the conference to apply collective intervention as contemplated in the Rio Treaty and in the anticommunist resolution of Caracas. If this is not possible, it could at least ask for the isolation of the Castro regime.

However, if the other Latin-American republics were induced either to isolate or quarantine or to break diplomatic and trade relations with the Castro regime, it would not in the long run prevent the realization of Castro's aims in Latin America. As to the stability of the Castro regime, the U.S.S.R., Red China, and the European satellites would take up enough of the slack to tide Castro over any economic damage that might occur. It is worth pointing out that the trade of the Cuban government with Latin America is negligible.

4. *Blockade.* A total sea and air blockade could prove quite effective but would be as risky as direct military intervention. It would be a war measure. Blockading ships must operate either outside the three-mile limit—thereby violating international law regarding free use of the high seas—or must intrude into the coastal waters where Cuba is sovereign. The stopping of a Russian tanker or freighter would bring more complications with the Soviet Union than direct military intervention in Cuba.

5. *Direct military intervention.* The military destruction of the Castro regime is the most effective way to save the Americas from communist domination and enslavement. This could be done by direct United States military intervention, by another invasion by Cuban exiles, or by joining with the other Latin hemispheric governments in a military effort.

Should the United States be unable to get the two-thirds majority in the OAS, its only alternative would be to act alone or through another paramilitary operation in which the Cuban exiles now serving in the United States armed forces would participate. Both the American people and the anti-

Castro Cubans are overwhelmingly in favor of the military approach. White House mail runs about four to one for military intervention in Cuba.

As far as the Cuban refugees are concerned, all émigré organizations, including Ray's leftist group, are now convinced that only U.S. military intervention can overthrow the Castro regime. The landing at Bahía de Cochinos proved that Castro has more than enough modern arms and men to repel anything but a full-scale invasion by the United States. Another invasion by Cuban exiles, unless given all-out support by U.S. military forces, would fail. The cold and efficient manner in which Castro's intelligence service rounded up more than 200,000 Cubans marked for detention by an organized system of informers belied the theory that the island would rise in revolt against the regime at the first sound of gunfire. Men simply do not revolt when they are looking down the muzzle of a machine gun.

Summarizing, the dominant mood of the Cuban people, almost three years after Castro came to power, has changed from enthusiasm to grimness. There is no doubt that the increased shortage of food and the regime's ironclad methods have cost Fidel some of his popularity among the underprivileged. He has, however, a huge body of active supporters and there does not seem to be any immediate internal threat to the continuance of his regime. The underground organizations that have been carrying out terrorism and sabotage against the Castro regime for many months were badly shaken by the extremely harsh measures that followed the invasion fiasco.

For the United States the Cuban case poses complex problems. Whatever Fidel Castro's ideological viewpoint, the fact is that he has avowedly committed himself to turning Cuba into a communist state. Che Guevara admitted to Latin-American diplomats at the Alliance for Progress meeting at Punta del Este, that the regime in Cuba is communist. "Cuba is communistic, but if you really want a constructive 'Alliance for Progress,' then let all the countries of the world participate, including the socialist bloc," Guevara stated.

The appearance of a communist state in Cuba might not of itself cause concern to the United States. Yet the Castro regime is not merely a communist dictatorship; it is a Soviet wedge in the Western Hemisphere to increasing world tensions, undermining the inter-American regional system, and carrying forward the cold war against the free world. Khrushchev and the Communist Chinese leaders not only support the Cuban revolution but openly espouse it as a pattern that should be applied to all of Latin America. As early as May of 1960 Khrushchev said:

> I can but welcome the events in Cuba, where the people proudly and courageously rose up under the banner for the struggle for their independence. I am convinced that other Latin-American countries also will rise up in the struggle against imperialism and colonialism.

There is little doubt that the historical role assigned to the Castro regime by the governments of the Soviet Union and the People's Republic of China is to conquer Latin America for international communism disguised under the old and now familiar slogan of "anti-imperialism" and "nationalism." As far as Fidel Castro is concerned, the Cuban leader is determined to go down in history as a twentieth-century Simón Bolívar, who "freed Latin America from Yankee imperialism."

If this is the role of Castro's Cuba in the worldwide strategy of international communism, it would be monstrous to permit a semantic preoccupation to interfere with whatever course is necessary to overthrow the present Cuban government. Khrushchev knows perfectly well that the United States cannot tolerate this situation in Cuba, any more than the Soviet Union could tolerate an American-dominated regime in Poland or any other country of the Soviet orbit.

It is hoped that a solution to the Castro threat can be found somewhere between direct intervention by the United States and a collective attempt by the United States and other Latin-American countries.

The question is, do we have the time and the ability to bring about a collective attempt to overthrow Castro or must the United States take the lone risk and launch a military invasion of Cuba?

The stakes are much too high merely to sit by and hope that all will go well.

Index

Union of Soviet Socialist Republics: aid to Cuba, 6, 54-55, 210; experts in, 53-54, 148-49; arms buildup, see arms; and Cuban economy, 72-73, 94, 105-7; attacks US, 121-22; in Mexico, 129; and Brazil, 133; use of Cuba, 170; intervention, in W. Hemisphere, 213, 229. See also war

United Nations: General Assembly of, 55; Castro at, 119; and invasion, 185

United States: appeal for aid to, 4; prestige of, 5-6; and Cuban arms, 57; and Cuban communism, 60-61; and Cuban economy, 72-73, 106, 107; nonrecognition of, 115; in Venezuela, 122, 127; and Bolivia, 128; and Mexico, 130; and Brazil, 130, 133, 135; and Colombia, 137; accused in Dominican crisis, 138; and anti-Castro measures, 141-42; invites Cuban children, 160; threatened by Cuba, 195-96; mistakes in Cuba, 195-214; congratulates Castro, 208; accused, 209-10; realignment of policy, 216, 219-20. See also anti-US entries, intervention

United States aid, to Latin America, 21. See also Alliance for Progress

United States Central Intelligence Agency (CIA), 112, 156; and invasion, 170, 172, 174-76, 178-81, 183, 184; opposes Ray, 187; and failure of invasion, 188, 189, 191-92; rightist leaning of, 193. See also Democratic Revolutionary Front

United States corporations, in Cuba, 64

United States Department of State: charges Cuban rearmament, 122; attitude toward Castro, 171, 198-99, 200, 211; attitude toward invasion, 183; and intervention, 201, 205; and Batista, 205-6; and training missions, 207

United States exports, to Cuba, 72

United States foreign policy: attacked, 16, 195-96; choices of, toward Cuba, 222-28

Urban Reform Law, 10

Urrutia, Manuel, Cuban president, 8, 18, 44, 45; fired, 23-24, 50

Vargas, Getulio, 133, 134

Varona, Manuel A. de, 65-66, 68, 132, 151, 173-74, 175, 179-81, 192, 201

vehicles, goal for, 100

Velasco Ibarra, José María, Ecuadorian president, 137-38

Venezuela, 201; Castro in, 122-27; riots in, 125, 128

Vital Minimum (V.M.), 86

wage increases, 74

war, Russo-US, 17-18, 21, 209, 215

Warsaw Pact, and Cuba, 55, 219

Western Hemisphere, defense of, 20; communism in, 63; Castro's revolution in, 115; Soviet intervention in, 213

White Rose group, 144

Wieland, William A., state department official, 200, 201

World Bank, 19

Ydigoras, Miguel Fuentes, Guatemalan president, 120

youth, indoctrination of, 158

youth farm, 91